FACING

TOMORROW

A Woman's Journey of Hope and Healing

TONYA JONES

Ordering Information:

Quantity sales. Special discounts are available on quantity purchases by corporations, associations, and others. For details, contact the publisher at the email address above.

Orders by U.S. trade bookstores and wholesalers.

Library of Congress Control Number: 2025926601

ISBN: 978-1-966612-99-5

Cover Design: Olaniyan Bukola

First Printed Edition: January 2026

Printed in the United States of America

Table of Contents

INTRODUCTION

"Grief is like the ocean; it comes in waves, ebbing and flowing. Sometimes the water is calm, and other times it crashes over you, pulling you under, leaving you gasping for breath."

As I sit here, reflecting on the past decade of my life, I can't help but feel the weight of the memories that shape my existence. Ten years ago, I lost my husband, the love of my life, my anchor in a world that suddenly felt so unsteady. I remember that day vividly. It was bright and sunny, an ordinary day that turned into the darkest moment of my life. Losing him was like losing a part of myself, a piece that I would never be able to retrieve.

Two years ago, my beloved son followed him into the unknown, a loss so incomprehensible that it turned my heart into a hollow chamber. Each day since May 4, 2023, has been a battle against the shadows of despair that threaten to engulf me. The laughter we shared, the dreams we built, all crumbled to dust, leaving behind an ache that is both familiar and foreign.

Just a year ago, I faced another devastating blow: the passing of my mother. She was my guiding light, my source of comfort, and losing her felt like losing my last tether to the life I once knew. The void left in her absence is an ever-present reminder of how fragile life can be, how quickly everything can change.

In writing this book, I aim to shed light on my journey through this labyrinth of grief. It's a story woven with threads of heartache and hope, a testament to the strength we didn't know we possessed until we were faced with unimaginable loss. My hope is that by sharing my experiences, the raw, unfiltered pain and the moments of unexpected joy, I can reach out to others who find themselves navigating their own dark waters.

I invite you, dear reader, to walk alongside me on this journey. It's not just my story. It's a shared human experience of love, loss, and resilience. Together, we will explore the strength that lies within us, waiting to be discovered amidst the chaos of life.

PROLOGUE

It was just another ordinary day, or so I thought. My husband had been working tirelessly, pushing himself harder than ever, and I noticed he wasn't quite himself. As a nurse, I recognized the signs. He seemed fatigued, and his laughter was slightly off-key. I suggested he go to the hospital, but he insisted, "Baby, just go ahead and go to work. Once I finish my work, I'll call you, and we can go together."

But that call never came. Instead, I received a message that filled my heart with unease. "I'm not feeling any better. Can you meet me at the truck stop?"

Rushing there, my instincts kicked in. The moment I laid my eyes on him, a surge of dread washed over me. He just didn't look right. In that instant, the nurse in me took over. I checked his vitals. His oxygen levels were low, and his heart rate was far from normal. I realized with chilling clarity that we had to get to the hospital.

"Can I go home and shave first?" he asked, his concern for appearances evident even in that moment of crisis. I took his chin gently, forcing him to meet my gaze. "No. We need to go now."

His breathing grew labored as I drove to the nearest emergency care clinic, every second feeling like an eternity. After what felt like hours of waiting, I saw the worry etched in the doctor's eyes. It mirrored my own. They decided he needed to be transferred to the hospital, and as we wheeled him through the corridors, the gravity of our reality began to sink in.

I entered the hospital holding his hand, whispering words of comfort and love, but I left an entirely different person, empty and shattered, my heart breaking as he passed within 24 hours of being admitted.

This was just the beginning of my harrowing journey through grief, one that would bring me to the brink as I faced not only the loss of my husband but other unimaginable heartaches that followed.

In sharing my story, I hope to connect with others who have experienced similar heartaches. Together, we can find solace in the shared human experience of loss and resilience amid despair.

CHAPTER 1

The Day Everything Changed

"The Lord is close to the brokenhearted and saves those who are crushed in spirit." -Psalm 34:18 (NIV)

The sterile smell of the hospital still stayed with me as I left, a suffocating reminder of the life I had just lost. My hands trembled as I gripped the steering wheel, the hum of the engine drowned out by the storm of emotions moving inside me. Despair, disbelief, and an unbearable sense of emptiness washed over me, pulling me into a chasm I feared I would never escape.

The world outside continued as if nothing had happened. Birds chirped. People hurried along the sidewalks. The sun shone brightly, mocking the darkness that filled my chest. How could everything look the same when my whole life had just collapsed? The bright colors of the flowers lining the streets felt cruel, their beauty clashing with the hollowness inside me. I wanted to scream at the world to stop, to acknowledge my pain, to understand that everything had changed and that it no longer held meaning. But I could not.

Once home, I stood frozen at the doorway, staring into a space that felt unfamiliar and hollow. The warmth of our shared memories followed me inside. Every room carried echoes of his laughter. Every corner held traces of our love. His favorite chair. The kitchen where we cooked together. The photographs that captured brief moments of joy, now reduced to reminders I could not escape. I could almost hear his voice teasing me about my cooking or laughing at my terrible jokes. The silence inside the house pressed in on me. My ears strained to hear his voice one more time. My body ached to feel his embrace one last time. The realization that there would be no more moments with him settled heavily over me.

In the days that followed, I moved through grief without direction. I reached for my phone, my heart racing as I called my son at work. The call felt unreal. I told him to come to the hospital. I told him his father needed him. I struggled to communicate the weight of what was happening. I did not know how to share the devastation I felt. The words felt heavy as I spoke them. Each one landed with effort. Tears ran down my cheeks, but my voice remained steady. I needed to be strong for my son.

When he arrived, I caught a glimpse of his worried expression as he rushed through the hospital doors. I will never forget that moment. He stood there, vulnerable yet determined, as he moved toward me. He arrived just in time. The look in his eyes reflected my own fear and confusion, mirroring the storm inside us both. In that moment, we were united in grief in a way I cannot fully explain.

As we drove home together, the silence between us felt heavy, broken only by the sound of his slow, steady breathing. My heart ached for him, and for us, caught in a reality I could barely accept. When we arrived home, my son gently helped me into bed and sat beside me on the floor. We said nothing. In that quiet, I felt the depth of our bond as mother and son.

He held my hand tightly, as if trying to keep me anchored to this world while everything inside me fell apart. In the dim light of the room, we cried together, our tears moving freely in the silence. It was a release. An acknowledgment of the pain we shared. In that moment, I understood that grief was not mine alone to carry. It was something we would face together, shaped by the love that connected us.

Throughout our lives, my husband had been the steady presence in our family. He had a way of making even ordinary moments feel meaningful. I remember evenings spent cooking together in our kitchen, his laughter filling the space as we talked about the day. Those simple routines shaped our life as a family. Now, that sense of stability was gone, leaving us to move through a world that felt unfamiliar and difficult to face.

As I lay in bed staring at the ceiling, moments from our life together moved through my mind. Our wedding day. Our first date. Lazy Sunday mornings filled with warmth and laughter. Each memory felt fragile and sharp, beautiful but painful, pressing into my chest. I could almost feel his hand in mine. The warmth of his embrace. The way he pulled me close and whispered words that made the rest of the world fall away. Those moments were gone now, leaving behind a quiet absence that followed me through the night.

My son stayed with me, watching over me in silence. The weight of grief showed clearly on his young face. Though he was my child, in that moment I felt like the one who needed support. I wished I could protect him from this pain, even as I knew grief was something none of us could avoid.

In the midst of our tears, something shifted. A new sense of connection formed in that moment, shaped by shared sorrow and quiet strength. Together, we honored the memory of a remarkable man, someone who had shown us the true meaning of love, laughter, and resilience. We were not only mourning a loss. We were recognizing a life that had deeply influenced us, a life that had shaped who we had become.

As the night continued, I listened to the faint sound of my son breathing, a reminder that even in the darkness, something steady remained between us. We were moving into unfamiliar territory, but we were not alone. The connection we shared held us steady and carried us through the heavy weight of grief.

As I began this unexpected experience of loss, I understood it was only the beginning. What lay ahead would bring deeper pain and further tests of endurance. Each step forward reflected our strength, a movement not only through grief, but toward healing and hope. I knew the road ahead would be difficult, yet it also held the possibility of something new taking shape.

CHAPTER 2

When Love Was Laid To Rest

"Blessed are those who mourn, for they will be comforted."-Matthew 5:4

Planning my husband's funeral felt unreal, as if I were observing my life from the outside, watching someone else make decisions I was not ready to make. I moved through those days on autopilot—answering questions, signing papers, hearing words that barely registered. My body was present, but my heart floated somewhere else, caught between disbelief and a pain so deep it stole my breath. This was not how our story was meant to unfold. I was unprepared to choose caskets and songs, to confront a goodbye I never imagined having to say.

Amid the planning, a question rose within me, one I could no longer hold back. I whispered it to God, my voice cracking under the weight of grief. Why did you not warn me? Why did you not prepare me for this? I was not angry, only desperate. I needed to understand how my life could unravel so completely.

And in the quiet of that moment, I heard it. Not loud. Not dramatic. Just clear and steady.

I did.

Those two words stopped me.

Before I could question them, my mind moved back to a moment I had not revisited in years. It was July of 2014. I was planning a birthday celebration for my husband, excited, as always, to do something meaningful for him. October was approaching, and I was already thinking through the details. As I spoke about the party, he looked at me with a seriousness that made me pause. Then, calmly and without hesitation, he said he was not going to live to see his birthday.

I did not want to hear that. I refused to hear it. I dismissed his words immediately, brushing them aside as fear or something spoken in passing. I told him not to talk like that. I shut the conversation down because I was not ready—ready to imagine life without him, ready to face something so final. Love made it impossible to accept what my heart could not bear to lose.

Just two months later, in September 2014, he was gone.

Standing there now, planning his funeral, that moment returned with a force that stole my breath. The Holy Spirit had carried me straight back—gently, unmistakably. I realized then that the warning had been given. I simply had not been ready to receive it. The weight of that understanding settled over me, not with condemnation, but with sorrow. Sometimes preparation comes quietly, and sometimes love makes us deaf to what we cannot bear to imagine.

As if the pain of losing him were not enough, those days were marked by betrayal—things I never expected, people I never thought could hurt us. Instead of being allowed to grieve, I was forced into survival mode. I had to protect myself. I had to protect my family. There was no space to fall apart, no room to sit with my sorrow. Strength was required, even when my heart was breaking.

Amid it all, my family never left my side. My mother, my brother, and my sister-in-law stepped in without hesitation, becoming the foundation I had not realized I would need. They were my constant: steady, present, unwavering. When I could not think clearly, they helped me make decisions. When I felt like I might collapse under the weight of it all, they stood beside me and held me up. In a time when everything felt uncertain and fragile, they were my rock.

After my husband passed, I found myself going to the funeral home every morning. It became something my heart needed. I would take my coffee with me, just as I used to when he was home and not working. Coffee had always been our ritual: quiet mornings, shared glances, comfortable silence. Even in death, I could not let that routine go.

I would sit there with him, coffee in hand, letting the stillness wash over me. I talked to him, sometimes in my heart, sometimes out loud. I told him how much I loved him, how much I missed him, how unreal everything felt without him. Those mornings were both comforting and unbearable. Love does not stop when life does, and I felt that truth in every sip, every breath, every tear that fell in that quiet space.

The day of the funeral arrived with a finality I had been trying not to face. Everything moved too fast and too slow at the same time. People hugged me, spoke to me, and offered words meant to comfort, but their voices felt distant, as though I were underwater. I nodded when expected and responded when necessary, but my focus stayed on one thing: him.

Before the service, I was given a moment alone. I walked toward the casket on trembling legs, each step feeling like a goodbye I was not ready to take. When I reached him, I stood quietly, memorizing what I already knew I would never see again. This was the man I had built my life with. My safe place. My love.

I laid my head gently on his chest, and everything I had been holding inside finally broke loose. I cried from a place deeper than tears, from a part of my soul that had been broken open. I begged time to stop. I begged God for just one more moment. I pressed my face against him, wishing with everything in me that love alone could wake him.

I kissed him one last time and stayed there, because I knew, fully knew, that this was the end. There would be no more mornings together. No more shared coffee. No more laughter filling our home. This was the final goodbye, and it felt unbearable.

When it was time to close the casket, my heart screamed in protest. Every part of me wanted to stop it, to refuse to let the lid separate me from him forever. As it closed, a heaviness settled over me that I cannot fully put into words. In that moment, the truth became unavoidable. I would never see him again in this life.

That was when love was laid to rest.

Afterward, I stood there, my body present but my heart somewhere else. The service continued. Words were spoken. Prayers were offered. I felt my family close to me, steady and protective, holding me together when I no longer knew how to do that myself. Even surrounded by people, I had never felt such loss.

As the room emptied and the day came to an end, exhaustion settled into my bones. Love had been honored, a life remembered, and yet I knew this was not the end of my grief. It was the beginning of learning how to carry it.

When love was laid to rest, I walked away changed, holding onto faith, family, and memories, trying to figure out how to take the next step forward. I did not know how I would survive what lay ahead. I only knew that I had to keep moving, even if it was one breath at a time.

The world would continue. Time would keep passing. And I would have to learn how to live in the wake of loss.

CHAPTER 3

In the Wake of Loss

"For no one is cast off by the Lord forever. Though he brings grief, he will show compassion, so great is his unfailing love." -Lamentations 3:31–32 (NIV)

The days after the funeral blurred together, each one pressing down on me like a weight I did not yet know how to carry. The world kept moving forward, indifferent to the fact that mine had been altered. I existed somewhere between exhaustion and disbelief, learning moment by moment what it meant to live in the wake of loss.

After my husband's passing, the days continued to blur, each one adding pressure to my chest. Time felt distorted, stretching and contracting in ways that left me disoriented. I moved through the motions of life half present in a world that continued without him. The silence in our home was overwhelming, broken only by the echo of my thoughts, repeating the same truth. He was gone.

In the weeks that followed, I was inundated with condolences. Friends and family came through our door, offering meals, hugs, and words of comfort. Their kindness was genuine, yet it often felt like a thin veil over the raw wound of my grief. I appreciated their intentions, but the ache in my heart made it difficult to connect fully. I felt separate from it all, aware of their presence but unable to step back into the world they were trying to support me in.

My son, still processing the loss, became my anchor amid overwhelming emotion. I watched him move through his own grief, trying to protect me while quietly needing reassurance himself. The nights we spent crying together gave way to long stretches of silence, heavy with what neither of us knew how to say. I could see the burden he carried, the worry visible on his young face, the way he often pulled inward. As his mother, it was painful to realize that I could not take that weight from him.

One afternoon, as I sat staring at a photo of our family, my son approached me with hesitation. "Mama, do you think... do you think Dad would want us to be sad forever?" His question landed deeply, moving through the quiet spaces I had been avoiding. In that moment, I felt the weight of our grief pressing down on us. My sense of happiness felt tied to his, and his to mine.

"I do not know, sweetheart," I said, my voice unsteady. "But I think it is okay to be sad. It is okay to miss him. We just have to find a way to remember him and to honor the love we shared."

The words stayed with us, creating a moment of connection in the middle of our grief. It became clear that while we had lost someone central to our lives, we still carried his love with us. It remained present, even as we struggled to move forward.

As the days turned into weeks, I began to look for comfort in memory. I started a journal, using the page as a place to organize what grief had disrupted. I wrote about my husband's laughter, the way he made ordinary moments feel meaningful, and the memories that brought both smiles and tears. Each entry became a quiet refusal to let loss take full control of my inner world.

I also began taking short walks, allowing the world outside to pull me back into motion. With each step, I felt as though I was honoring his memory, carrying him with me as I slowly reclaimed parts of my life. I walked through the park where we once spent long afternoons, the sound of children nearby reminding me of the joy we shared. Those early attempts at healing were uncertain, and the path ahead felt intimidating, but they were still forward steps.

I did not yet know that the next chapter of my life would bring challenges I had not anticipated, losses that would test my resilience and reveal strength I did not know I had.

I often paused, overwhelmed by memories that surfaced without warning. His laughter. The way he wrapped his arms around me. The steady comfort of his presence. I learned to let those moments exist, allowing the tears to come without resistance. They reflected the depth of the love we shared and reminded me that joy had once lived fully in our home. I would sit on the porch, watching the world move past, and allow the memories to settle.

My son would sometimes join me, and together we shared stories about his dad, laughing through the tears. It became something we returned to, a way of keeping him present in our lives. We talked about the small things he did, the way he danced in the kitchen, how he always knew how to make us smile, even during the hardest days.

As the seasons changed, so did I. I began to notice the small details: a blooming flower, the sound of laughter in the distance, the warmth of the sun on my skin. I realized that while the pain of loss would remain with me, it did not have to define me. I could carry my husband's love forward, letting it guide me as I navigated this new chapter of my life.

With each passing day, a flicker of hope grew within me. I was learning to live again, to embrace the moments of joy that coexisted with my grief. I began to notice small signs of life around me: the way leaves moved in the wind, the laughter of children playing in the park, the warmth of a stranger's smile. These moments, once overshadowed by sorrow, gradually became part of my daily experience.

I reached out to friends I had not spoken to in some time, sharing my journey with them. Their support became a lifeline, a reminder that I was not alone in this struggle. We gathered for coffee, exchanged stories, and shared laughter, and I felt the weight of my grief ease, if only briefly.

One evening, as my son lay in bed, he turned to me and asked, "Mom, do you think Dad is watching us?"

I looked at the young man beside me, and tears filled my eyes. I paused, the question hanging between us, delicate and uncertain.

"I believe he is, sweetheart," I said, gently patting his forehead. "I think he is always with us, in our hearts and in our memories."

His face brightened with a small smile. He held my hand and closed his eyes. In that moment, I felt a surge of warmth— a reminder that love can endure even the deepest losses.

As the months passed, I began to embrace the idea of creating new traditions in my husband's honor. We started a family night every Friday, cooking his favorite meals and sharing stories about him. It became a space for us to remember, to laugh, and to cry together.

Through it all, I learned that grief is not a linear path. It ebbs and flows, sometimes crashing over me like a wave, other times retreating to reveal the shore beneath. I learned to ride those waves, to let them wash over me without losing myself in the depths.

CHAPTER 4

Echoes of Love

"We are hard pressed on every side but not crushed." - 2 Corinthians 4:8

At the time of his father's passing, my son was only 19, an age still filled with dreams and possibilities. He often looked like his father, with the same mischievous sparkle in his eyes that could light up a room. It was a bittersweet reminder of what we had lost, but also a source of comfort, evidence that our love had created something enduring. As my son grew, I noticed traces of his father in his mannerisms, his laughter, and his determination to succeed against all odds.

I did my best to keep my husband's spirit alive in our home. I shared cherished stories from our lives together, filling our conversations with laughter as we revisited moments when everything felt whole. We cooked his favorite meals, letting the aroma fill the kitchen. Each dish was a tribute to the man who had shaped our lives. The kitchen became a sanctuary, a place where memories and food coexisted, and every meal honored his life.

I remember the annual trips we took as a family. My husband told tall tales about the creatures in the woods while my son squealed with laughter, his joy contagious. Those memories became part of our lives, a record of love and adventure. With each story retold, I hoped to pass on his wisdom and warmth, even in his absence. I wanted my son to know his father not just through words, but through the love that remained in our home.

One morning, as we prepared breakfast—one of his favorites—I recounted the first time my son had attempted to make pancakes for him. "I remember the kitchen was a disaster. He spilled flour everywhere. I laughed so hard I nearly cried," I said, smiling at the memory. My son's eyes widened with amusement, and for the first time, I saw the joy in his face—the way he smiled in that moment, reflecting the happiness his father had brought into our lives.

"Did Dad really say he would never eat my cooking again?" he teased, a look of mock horror on his face, his laughter filling the room.

"Only until you learned to cook properly!" I replied with a laugh, our shared memory serving as a balm for our souls. In those moments, the weight of grief felt lighter, and the bond between us grew stronger.

Despite these moments of joy, struggles remained beneath the surface. As my son navigated his early twenties, I noticed a change—a withdrawal that reflected the grief we both carried but seldom spoke of. The wounds of loss were still present beneath his bravado, and the absence of his father began to show in ways that concerned me. I could see shadows of doubt creeping into his once bright spirit.

He faced challenges that felt insurmountable. The world seemed more complicated without his father's guidance, a presence who would have counseled him through life's hurdles. I often watched my son wrestle with decisions that had once been simple, each choice burdened by the weight of loss. The laughter that once filled our home was often replaced by silence, a silence that spoke to the grief we were both navigating.

He was forced to make decisions about his future, yet the excitement of those milestones was overshadowed by the void left by his father. I would catch him staring into space, a distant look in his eyes, as if grappling with the magnitude of the choices ahead. It broke my heart to see him struggle, to witness the weight of his father's absence pressing down on his young shoulders.

"Mom, do you think I'm making the right choices?" my son asked one night, his voice thick with uncertainty. The question cut deep, and I wanted nothing more than to give him the clarity and guidance his father would have offered. I felt the ache in my heart as I searched for the right words to comfort him.

"You're doing your best, honey. That's all anyone can ask for," I replied, though part of me wished I could assure him that everything would be okay, that we would be okay. I wanted to wrap him in the warmth of my love and shield him from the pain of loss, but I knew that was impossible.

On some evenings, when the weight of grief felt especially heavy, I found myself talking to my husband as if he were still there. "What would you say to him?" I would whisper into the stillness of the room, hoping for a sign, a word of guidance from the man I loved. Those moments of solitude became a bridge to the past, reminding me of our shared love even in his absence. I would close my eyes and imagine his voice, his laughter, and the way he would have reassured our son.

Though my husband's physical presence had faded, the love he shared with us remained a guiding force, shaping who we were becoming. While I held onto his memory, I now had to confront my own fears and insecurities as a mother. I wanted so desperately for my son to flourish, to navigate life's challenges with the guidance his father could no longer provide. I often questioned whether I was enough to fill the void left by him.

As I reflected on these complexities, I understood that our journey through grief was not just about mourning what we had lost. It was about finding a way to honor that love and carry it forward, even amid the new challenges ahead. I realized that grief was not a linear path but a winding road with unexpected turns and moments of clarity.

Little did I know, the road was about to fork again, leading me into uncharted territory I had never expected.

CHAPTER 5

Navigating New Waters

*"When you pass through the waters, I will be with you... they will not sweep over you." - **Isaiah 43:2 (NIV)***

As the seasons turned, life began to settle into a new rhythm, yet the current of grief remained ever-present. I learned to navigate my days without my husband, though the path was rarely straight. Each morning reminded me of his absence, and I often reached for the phone to share mundane updates with him, only to remember I could no longer call.

My son was adjusting to life after high school, torn between the excitement of new opportunities and the heavy weight of his father's absence. This period should have been a thrilling adventure, yet it quickly became a tumultuous ride. While he eagerly sought new friends and experiences, I could see the toll grief exacted on him with every passing day.

"Mom, it's hard to make connections when everyone is so carefree," he admitted one evening, his voice thick with frustration. I watched his shoulders sag, the sparkle that once danced in his eyes reduced to a faint flicker. It broke my heart to see him struggle, feeling isolated among new faces, all seemingly untouched by loss. I wished I could shield him from the pain, but I knew that was impossible.

"It's natural to feel that way, sweetheart. It takes time," I said, hoping to offer comfort. My own heart ached as I realized how much he needed his father's guidance during this critical period, a mentor who would have encouraged him to explore his passions and find his own path. I longed to fill that void, yet I felt unequipped to do so.

At home, dinner became a bittersweet ritual. We sat together at the table, the remnants of our previous lives hanging awkwardly in the air. Conversation often felt strained, broken by long silences that echoed my husband's absence. The chair across from us, once filled with his presence, served as a stark reminder of what we had lost. I often paused mid-sentence, searching for echoes of laughter that once filled our home, wishing for just one more moment of normalcy.

One evening, as I served dinner, I noticed my son pushing food around his plate, lost in thought. I summoned the courage to ask, "Do you want to talk about your new job?" It was a gentle nudge, a small attempt to draw him out of his shell. I hoped that by opening the door, he might feel safe enough to step through.

"It's fine," he replied, his tone dismissive. Yet I could sense the burden he carried. The pressures, combined with the sorrow of navigating the world without his father, felt like an insurmountable wall. I wanted to break through that wall, to help him find a way to express what he was feeling.

In his grief, my son found solace at my husband's grave. He often brought flowers, kneeling to speak to his father and sharing snippets of his life—the challenges he faced, accomplishments he was proud of, and the daily joys and sorrows that filled his days. Sometimes, I would catch him sitting silently, tears rolling down his cheeks as he grappled with the weight of his emotions.

"Dad, it's so hard without you," I imagined him saying, a weak smile breaking through his tears. "I wish you were here to see it." These moments of vulnerability became vital for him, a way to express feelings he struggled to voice elsewhere. I could see him transforming the cemetery into a sanctuary, a place where he could lay his heart bare, free from judgment or expectation. It was a bittersweet comfort, but it was his way of keeping his father's memory alive.

On weekends, we tried to establish new traditions— simple outings to the park or an occasional movie night—but the joy felt different. I could sense my son holding back, the weight of grief pulling him down even during moments meant for connection. "Can we not talk about Dad tonight?" he would sometimes say, and I understood. Grief can be exhausting. Sometimes it felt easier to bury it beneath the surface, to pretend for just a little while that everything was okay.

During those trying months, support from friends sometimes felt like a warm blanket, and at other times, like an unwanted reminder of our loss. While they meant well, phrases like "He's in a better place" or "Time heals all wounds" felt hollow against the reality we faced. I appreciated their efforts, yet I often longed for a deeper understanding of what I was truly feeling—the complex layers of love and loss that colored my daily existence. Articulating my grief, even to those who cared, was a struggle.

One day, a close friend invited me to a grief support group. Hesitant but curious, I decided to give it a chance. Walking into the room was daunting. The walls felt heavy with unspoken pain. I was greeted by a circle of faces marked by shared sorrow, each story unique yet strangely familiar. As I listened to others recount their experiences, I felt an undeniable bond. We were all navigating turbulent waters, longing for understanding and connection. It was a relief to know I was not alone in my feelings.

Sharing my own journey felt liberating, a release I had not realized I needed. I spoke about my husband—the laughter, the love, the dreams we had once shared, and the dreams now shattered. The group members nodded in understanding, their eyes reflecting the same ache I felt inside. It was a moment of solidarity, a reminder that grief, while isolating, could also bring people together.

"Grief is love that has nowhere to go," one member said during a meeting, and those words resonated deeply within me. I realized how desperately I had tried to protect my love for my husband, keeping it bottled up when it longed to be expressed. With every story shared, I felt walls breaking down, allowing space for healing. I began to understand that my love for him could coexist with my grief—that it was okay to let it flow freely.

I remember one woman sharing how she still set a place at the table for her late husband. "I talk to him while I eat," she said, her voice trembling with emotion. "It helps. It feels like he's still part of my world." I found comfort in her words and was inspired to create my own rituals that honored my love for my husband without being confined to silence. It was a small step, but it felt significant.

As I immersed myself in this healing journey, small moments of light began to emerge. Despite the heartache, I discovered strength I had not known existed within me. Each time I shared a memory of my husband with the group—his laughter, his dreams, his way of seeing the world—I felt a little more whole. I began to realize that sharing those memories was not just a way to remember him, but a way to keep his spirit alive.

But life remained unpredictable. One evening, as I sat on the couch with my son, I sensed a shift in the air. He had been unusually quiet, staring out the window as if seeking answers in the stars. I hesitated, struggling to find the right words without disturbing the fragile peace between us. The silence felt heavy, charged with unspoken thoughts and emotions.

"Are you okay?" I finally asked, my heart racing. He turned to me, his expression raw.

"No, Mom, I'm not okay. I miss him. I feel lost without him," he confessed, and my heart broke for him all over again. It took everything in me to hold back my tears. I wanted nothing more than to comfort him, yet I felt the same weight of grief pressing on my chest. In that moment, I realized we were navigating the same storm, each of us trying to find our way through the darkness.

"I miss him too," I admitted, my voice barely above a whisper. "But we have each other, and I'm here. We can talk about him whenever you want." It was a small promise, yet it felt significant—a commitment to face our grief together.

He nodded, and the fragile connection between us deepened. It was a moment of honesty, both a breakthrough and a reminder of the uncharted territory we were navigating. I knew the waves of grief were far from over, yet we were slowly learning to ride them, finding strength in our shared love and memories. As I looked at my son, I sensed the next wave approaching. I remained unprepared for the challenges it would bring, but I felt a glimmer of hope that we would face it together.

CHAPTER 6

Shadows of Doubt

"For the Spirit God gave us does not make us timid, but gives us power, love, and self-discipline." -2 Timothy 1:7 (NIV)

As the months slipped by, the weight of my husband's absence became an unshakable presence in our lives. While I had begun to find my footing in this new reality, I sensed my son teetering on the edge of his own emotional cliff. I often wondered if he felt the same heaviness I carried—a burden we shared.

His transition to a new job had begun with promise, but over time, I noticed changes that troubled me. His excitement faded into indifference. Where there had once been energy, I now observed hesitation. The phone calls that had once brought me joy became brief and clipped. Responses felt perfunctory, as if he were simply going through the motions. The vibrant colors of his life had dulled to shades of gray.

"Do you want to join me for an event this weekend?" I would ask, trying to bridge the growing gap between us.

"Nah, I've got stuff to do," he'd reply, the shadows under his eyes betraying sleepless nights, and my heart sank a little further. Every "I'm fine" that escaped his lips felt like a small dagger, a reminder of the pain I could not ease. I longed to reach through the distance and pull him back into connection.

One evening, as I cleaned up after dinner, I noticed his backpack lying untouched in the living room. Opening it, I found crumpled papers—letters he had written to Jibriel— evidence of the struggle he was facing. The realization hit me like a wave. He was drowning in emotions he could not express, and I feared he might be slipping further away. Each letter offered a glimpse into his heart, a heart too heavy to share.

Determined to reach him, I approached the subject gently. "You know, sweetheart, it's okay to ask for help if you're feeling overwhelmed. You're not alone in this."

"I don't need help, Mom. I just need to focus," he snapped, frustration rising to the surface. His words stung, but I understood they were a shield against the vulnerability he feared.

At that moment, I recognized the familiar spark of anger hidden within his grief—the anger at a world that continued without his father, a world that could not grasp the depth of his ache. I wanted to shake him and tell him it was perfectly okay to not be okay, but instead, I offered a soft smile. "Just remember, I'm here if you want to talk. I promise I won't judge."

Days turned into weeks, each one a battle against the tide of emotions threatening to pull us under. I felt helpless as I watched my son push me away, as if subconsciously protecting me from his pain. The truth was, I longed to be a sanctuary, something solid for him to lean on during the storm. I wished he could see that sharing his burden would lighten the load for both of us.

He continued to visit the cemetery frequently, often spending hours in quiet reflection. I found comfort in knowing he sought connection with his father, but my heart ached to see him place all his own emotions on that gravestone, as if it were the only outlet he felt safe using. Each visit was a silent conversation, a way for him to express what words could not.

One day, as I prepared dinner, I caught sight of him through the patio window, sitting on the grass with his head bowed, flowers scattered around as evidence of his visits to the cemetery. I silently wished I could be with him, to share that moment, to let him know he was not alone even in his solitude. Seeing him so lost in thought made me yearn to reach out and hold him close.

It occurred to me that he might need more than a mother. He needed a confidant, someone who could help him navigate this maze of grief. I began considering professional help—a therapist who could provide guidance and a safe space for my son to express the range of emotions weighing on him. The thought of a stranger helping him felt daunting, yet necessary.

At a dinner with friends one evening, the topic of mental health came up. I listened as they shared stories of seeking therapy and support for their families. My heart pounded at the thought. Could this be the key to easing my son's suffering? Their experiences resonated with me, sparking a flicker of hope.

That night, I approached the subject carefully. "How would you feel about seeing a counselor? Someone who can help you work through your feelings?"

He looked at me, eyes swimming with a mix of frustration and fear. "I don't need someone else to tell me how to feel, Mom. I can handle it." His defiance was a wall I could not breach, yet I recognized it was built from fear and pain.

His defensiveness echoed through me, and I fought the urge to push further. I understood that grappling with grief is an intensely personal journey. It could be exhausting and isolating. I chose patience instead, leaving the door open for future conversations. I hoped that one day he would see the value in sharing his burden with someone who could help.

Still, that worry gnawed at me. How long could I protect him from this storm? How long before the shadows eclipsed the light? Each day felt like a tightrope walk, balancing my desire to help with the need to respect his autonomy.

In those moments of reflection, I often thought about my husband his laughter, his counsel, and the way he navigated life's ups and downs with ease. Memories would flood my mind, bringing both warmth and sorrow. I wished he were here to guide us through this darkness, to remind us that it was okay to seek help.

One memory resurfaced as I flipped through old family albums. I found a picture of my husband teaching our son how to tie a tie. The triumphant smiles captured on film filled me with bittersweet nostalgia. "You got this, buddy! Just keep trying!" he had cheered, pride radiating from every pore. That moment captured the love and support that had always been at the core of our family.

As I stared at the image, I realized that grief, like riding a bike, is something you learn to navigate, even if you wobble along the way. But what happens when you struggle to pedal? I feared that without guidance, my son might fall—and I would not be there to catch him.

Little did I know that the challenges ahead would not only test my son's resilience but also my own, plunging us into uncharted waters where love, loss, and the fragility of life intertwined. The journey would demand strength from both of us, and I hoped we could find our way together.

CHAPTER 7

Facing Tomorrow

"They are new every morning; great is your faithfulness."
- Lamentations 3:23 (NIV)

The season of change had arrived, bringing a swirl of emotions, and I found myself caught in a whirlwind of uncertainty. As the leaves turned, I noticed a shift in both my son and me. While I had hoped the support group would offer tools for coping, I could see that facing each new day weighed heavily on him. Simply waking up seemed a challenge, and I sought to instill a sense of hope amidst the sorrow that surrounded us.

Cold mornings heralded the approach of winter and the holiday season. For many, this time was filled with joy and celebration, but for us, it served as a stark reminder of absence. The anticipation of family gatherings and festive traditions felt overwhelming, and I knew I had to tread carefully. The more I thought about it, the more I sank into memory. I could hear echoes of laughter we had once shared, amplifying the silence that now filled our home.

One afternoon, I wandered through a local store, the twinkling lights and holiday decorations casting a bittersweet glow over my heart. As I moved through the aisles, a display of ornaments and wreaths caught my eye. Among them was a simple wooden sign that read, "Home for the Holidays." For a fleeting moment, it evoked my husband's presence—the laughter, the shared stories, the love we had built as a family. But the truth quickly settled in, pressing heavily on my chest. We would not be whole this year, and the realization felt like a cold wave washing over me.

Returning home, I laid my purchases on the table, conflicted. "We need to create new traditions," I told my son that evening, hoping to spark a sense of possibility. "Maybe we can volunteer together during the holidays or have a small gathering to honor your father's memory." I believed that by doing something meaningful, we could begin to heal, though I was unsure if he would see it that way.

He looked up from his phone, skepticism etched across his face. "Mom, what's the point? He's not here. It won't be the same." His words struck a chord, stirring the deep grief we both carried. I could feel the frustration bubbling beneath the surface, yet I understood. The holidays were complicated. They amplified grief, trapping us in cycles of nostalgia and loss. "I know it won't be the same, but we can still honor him. We can carry his spirit forward in our own way."

His silence lingered, thick and heavy. I knew we needed to find a balance between remembering the past and embracing the present, yet convincing him to take that step felt daunting. It was a delicate dance, one that demanded patience and understanding.

As December approached, I suggested a holiday journal. "We can each write down our memories, our thoughts, and the things we loved about this time of year with him," I proposed. He looked skeptical but agreed to try, perhaps sensing my earnest desire to connect.

With each entry, we began to find small moments of connection. I reminisced about our family baking sessions— the scent of cookies filling the house, the laughter as flour flew across the kitchen. "Remember the time Jibriel covered your face with flour when you tried to help?" I chuckled, and a glimmer of a smile broke through my son's facade. It was a reminder that joy could still exist, even in the shadow of our grief.

"Yeah, I remember," he replied, a hint of nostalgia in his voice. It became a small victory, a moment where we stepped briefly out of grief to share a laugh. These shared memories drew us closer, reminding us of the love that remained.

During those nights spent journaling, I became increasingly aware of my own uncertainty. In the quiet hours, reflecting on my husband's absence, I felt anger and sadness swirling with budding determination. I wanted to emerge from this place of sorrow, to reshape my narrative and help my son do the same. It was a journey we had to undertake together, even if the path was unclear.

I reached out to friends in the support group, seeking advice on how to approach the holidays with intention. They shared strategies that had helped them navigate similar struggles, encouraging me to set boundaries while honoring the memory of loved ones. As their stories unfolded, I realized grief is not a linear path. It ebbs and flows, sometimes catching us off guard when we least expect it. This understanding gave me a sense of solidarity, reminding me that we were not alone.

As the days grew shorter and the holidays approached, my son agreed to join me in volunteering at a local shelter, an act that brought purpose to our days. On the first day, he showed initial reluctance, yet I saw sparks of hope as he interacted with families in need. The smiles and gratitude there began to light a flicker in his heart, piercing the darkness that had settled over us.

We prepared meals together, served hot food, and shared laughter with those we met. In those moments, I watched my son transform, the weight on his shoulders lifting just a little. He began to find joy in helping, discovering that giving back was a way to cope with his grief. Through service, he seemed to reclaim a part of himself that had been lost.

Yet even amid these moments of hope, reminders of loss surfaced. One evening, as we returned home from our volunteer shift, I noticed my son pausing at the front door. "Can we light a candle for him?" he asked, eyes glistening with unspilled tears. His request reminded me of the love that still connected us to his father.

"Of course we can," I replied, feeling a mix of pride and sorrow. We lit a candle together, watching the flame flicker in the darkness, a symbol of love enduring beyond loss. In that moment, I felt a sense of peace, knowing we were honoring his memory in a way that felt authentic.

As we stood in that quiet moment, I realized that while the holidays would never be what they once were, we were forging new paths, finding ways to honor my husband's memory and rediscover joy amid the pain. Together, we were slowly learning to embrace each day, drawing strength from the memories we cherished and the love that bound us. It was a journey of healing, one that required patience with ourselves and with each other.

Little did I know, the road ahead would soon lead us into another chapter, one filled with trials that would challenge our understanding of hope and the process of healing.

CHAPTER 8

Embracing the Holidays

*"There is a time for everything, and a season for every activity under the heavens." - **Ecclesiastes 3:1 (NIV)***

The holiday season arrived with a rush of activity, filling our home with lights and decorations that carried mixed emotions. As we hung ornaments together, I felt the weight of my husband's absence. Each ornament held a memory, a moment of laughter, joy, and togetherness from past holidays. Still, as I watched my son carefully place the star at the top of the tree, I noticed a small but meaningful shift. There was effort in his movement, a quiet intention that had been missing for some time.

"He always used to say the star shines the brightest, just like our family," my son said. A faint smile appeared before fading. "But it doesn't feel complete without him here." He looked at me, and the loss in his expression was unmistakable.

"I know, sweetheart," I said. The grief was familiar, steady, and present. "But we can honor him during this time. We carry him with us, and we still have each other." In that moment, I understood that grief and hope were not opposites. They existed together, shaping how we moved forward.

As Christmas approached, I felt the pressure of expectation, the urge to create joy while managing our sorrow. Family gatherings carried mixed emotions. Relatives offered love and support, yet the absence of my husband remained constant and inescapable. At times, the weight felt difficult to carry, but I knew I had to keep moving forward, for myself and for my son.

Despite the heaviness of our loss, my son showed steady resilience over the past year. He often carried a warm smile and found reasons to celebrate each day, especially after the birth of his son on August 3, 2020, a moment that reshaped his life. Becoming a father brought renewed purpose to him, helping him move through grief while deepening the love he held for his father and now for his child.

That new life brought a deeper understanding of legacy, not only what was lost but what could still be nurtured and carried forward. It served as a bittersweet reminder that life continues, holding space for memory while allowing room for growth.

On Christmas Eve, we gathered with family, surrounded by laughter and seasonal cheer. For a brief moment, it felt almost normal, as though forgetting were possible. Yet each time I looked around the room, the absence of my husband pressed in. He would have shifted the atmosphere, bringing a presence that could not be replaced.

After dinner, we sat together sharing stories. I spoke about family outings, and laughter filled the room. Talking about

Jibriel felt natural, and seeing others remember him with the same care I carried brought tears to my eyes. He was loved far more deeply than I had ever realized. I glanced at my son, who moved between moments of warmth and quiet reflection. The holidays reminded him of what he had lost, but also of what he had gained, a son who carried his name and extended his legacy.

As the evening continued, I suggested a toast to my husband. "To Jibriel," I said, lifting my glass. "To the love he shared, the laughter he brought, and the memories we will carry forward."

"To Jibriel," everyone echoed. I felt warmth rise from the shared remembrance, followed by the sharp ache of his absence. He had once been the center of our family. With quiet smiles and tear filled eyes, we carried on through the rest of the night.

The next day, we made our usual trip to the cemetery. My son held a bouquet of fresh flowers, his expression growing heavier as we approached the grave. "I miss you, Dad," he said softly, placing the flowers beside the headstone. "I have been trying. Life is hard. I wish you could help me."

Those moments at the cemetery are sacred, a space where sorrow and love meet without resistance. Words often fall short, yet they are all we have to bridge the distance between the living and the lost. I held my son close, aware of his quiet struggle and his longing for the guidance of a father who was no longer there.

I watched him, tears gathering in his eyes as he carried the weight of emotions too heavy for his age. In that moment, it became clear. I was not only grieving my husband. I was grieving the father son bond my son had been forced to lose. I stepped closer and wrapped my arm around him, offering presence rather than answers. "I know it's difficult," I said. "But you're doing great. He would be so proud of you."

Despite the heaviness of that moment, I could not ignore the joy my son had found in fatherhood. He often joked that becoming a dad had turned him into a "softie," a claim reinforced by the care and attention he gave his son. That love guided him forward and reminded him of the lessons Jibriel had shared. It gave him the strength to face college life and move through the layered emotions of grief.

At times, I reflected on how grief shapes people differently. It does not always break us. Sometimes it builds something unexpected. My son's quiet strength reflected that shift, a steady presence that held even during the hardest hours.

As the holidays unfolded, we adjusted to new traditions. We cooked together, sharing recipes tied to meals from earlier years, trying to recreate the warmth of family gatherings. Each night, we journaled side by side, recording memories we still carried while making room for new ones with his son.

Yet even with the comfort of new traditions, moments of deep sadness surfaced. New Year's Eve arrived, and as the clock moved closer to midnight, tension built inside me. The idea of stepping into a new year without my husband filled me with dread. Life was moving forward, while I remained anchored in grief.

We attended a small gathering. As the countdown began, I watched faces brighten with anticipation while my heart stayed heavy. When the clock struck midnight, cheers broke out. My son turned toward me, his eyes wet with emotion. "Happy New Year, Mom," he said quietly.

"Happy New Year, sweetheart," I replied, drawing him into an embrace. In that moment, I wanted to believe the year ahead could still hold healing and hope.

But just as a tentative sense of optimism began to form, everything shifted. It was the morning of May 4, 2023, the last time I spoke with my son. He had an important job interview that day, and we planned to meet afterward. I was in a meeting when I received a text from him: "Mama, I love you." I replied, "Baby, I love you too."

Later, my phone began to buzz with messages from his friends. A wave of concern moved through me as they reached out, asking if I had heard from him. As I looked at my phone, my heart started to race. Something was wrong.

In a panic, I called a close friend and asked him to go to my son's apartment immediately. "He hasn't answered his phone," I said, fear entering my voice. "I need you to check on him." My heart was pounding, as if bracing me for what was coming.

As I waited, dread spread through my body. When the call finally came, my world collapsed. "I'm so sorry," my friend said, his voice heavy. "The ambulance is leaving now. He didn't make it."

I had heard people say that words can build you or break you, but I never understood it until that moment. The weight of what he said hit all at once. In seconds, everything around me felt distorted. The holiday celebrations, the noise, the movement, all of it faded. I had lost my son, and the pain that followed was beyond understanding.

I dropped to my knees, my chest breaking apart. What had happened? The question repeated in my mind as tears fell without pause. I tried to stay quiet, to hold it in, but I could not. It was too much. All of it was too much for a mother.

The journey of hope and healing I had aimed to create for both of us had abruptly ended in the most devastating way possible, leaving an empty space where his laughter used to fill the air.

CHAPTER 9

A Legacy of Love

*"[God] comforts us in all our troubles, so that we can comfort those in any trouble." - **2 Corinthians 1:4 (NIV)***

In the days following my son's passing, the world felt unfamiliar. The holiday celebrations that once filled our home with laughter gave way to silence, leaving an emptiness that moved through every room. My grandson, only two years old, became a steady source of relief in those days. His presence brought moments of calm and light against the weight of grief that threatened to overtake us.

He was my son's center, shaped by the bond they shared. At times, it felt as though God understood he would need to grow quickly, carrying his father forward in ways no child should have to. Many in our family said a toddler would not remember the details of loss. Still, I found comfort in believing he carried parts of his father within him, held quietly, even if he could not yet give them words.

"Daddy," he would say with a smile, reaching for the photographs of my son placed around the house. Each time he pointed to them, I caught flashes of my son's laughter reflected in his child's bright eyes. The joyful sounds my son once drew from him were gone, replaced by quiet. Still, the bond between them remained, steady and unbroken in our lives.

Yet as much as my grandson brought comfort, he also deepened the ache of our loss. I often thought about the love my mother had for my son, her only grandson and the center of her heart. Their connection felt unshakable. You would have thought she had given birth to him herself. My mother adored him, holding close every moment and finding deep joy in being his grandmother. When she received the news of my son's passing, it was as if the ground beneath her gave way.

"Why him?" she whispered, her voice shaking with disbelief. "He was such a good man. He had so much to live for." Her grief reflected my own, raw and consuming. I could see her trying to stay strong for me, offering quiet support and steady hugs when the weight of sorrow became too much. Still, I knew she was hurting deeply. She had dedicated her life to raising my son and had dreamed of becoming a grandmother, a role she embraced fully. To see the center of her life taken away left a void that felt impossible to fill.

In our home, we began forming new routines, working with the love that remained. I took my grandson to the park, where he chased pigeons with an easy laugh, the sound calling back memories of my son's laughter from years before. Watching him play stirred both pain and warmth at once, a reminder of the love my son gave to fatherhood. I often drifted into thought, wondering what my son would have said or done in those moments, wishing I could hear his voice one more time.

As spring unfolded, I watched my grandson grow, just as I had hoped my son could have. I brought him to the cemetery regularly. His little feet bounded along the path, full of life. We would sit by my son's grave, sharing stories and memories. "Daddy is here, right, Nana?" he would ask, confusion crossing his small face.

"Yes, sweetheart," I replied, my voice soft but steady. He placed flowers at the grave, arranging them with care, and in those moments, it felt like we were bridging the gap left by grief. Holding him close, I felt a flicker of hope that love endures, even through the darkest circumstances.

Yet even amid these moments of comfort, the shadows of loss remained. My mother's initial strength began to fade as weeks turned into months. One evening, she confided, "I feel so lost without him, and I don't know how to help you." Her words lingered, a stark reminder of the fragility of our shared grief.

"Mother, it's okay to feel this way. We're both navigating this together. We'll honor him by supporting each other," I assured her, though I felt the weight of my own heart shattering at the thought of losing her support. Our family felt fragile, but I held onto the belief that we could rebuild it. The love we shared for my son—memories, stories, and care—became our lifeline, connecting us through the pain of loss.

As the sun set, casting a warm glow across the living room, I felt my grandson pressed against me as we flipped through the photo album I had filled with memories of my son. Each page was a journey through time, a collection of smiles and laughter that felt comforting and heartbreaking at once. I smiled through the tears, each drop a reminder of the love we had lost but continued to hold. "He would have adored you," I said softly, lifting my grandson's chin to meet my gaze, searching for the spark of my son in his eyes.

In that moment, I realized that while grief was a powerful tide threatening to pull us under, love would always be the lifeline we could hold onto. My son's memory would live on in the laughter of his child, in the stories we shared, and in the strength we drew from each other as we faced the future. I could almost hear my son's voice whispering through the pages of our memories, urging us to find moments of joy amid the sorrow.

CHAPTER 10

"Echoes of Loss"

*"Weeping may endure for a night, but joy comes in the morning." - **Psalm 30:5 (NIV)***

Losing my husband was a tragedy that shook the foundation of my life. It felt as if my soul had been ripped from my body, leaving an empty shell struggling to breathe. The life I knew—our life—collapsed in an instant, and I was left standing in the ruins, trying to comprehend how everything could vanish so quickly. For years, I fought through the darkness that followed, grappling with grief and searching for a path back to the light.

For nearly ten years, I survived one day at a time. Some days, I leaned heavily on my faith, believing God was the only reason I was still standing. Other days, faith felt distant, overshadowed by exhaustion and sorrow. Still, I held on. I learned to exist in a world without my husband, even when it felt unnatural and unfair. I learned to function while carrying a pain that never truly left.

Then, I lost my son.

When he died, the ground beneath me gave way once more, but this time, there was nothing left to steady me. The shock of his passing released a depth of despair I had never known, a grief that eclipsed everything that came before it. Losing my husband broke my heart. Losing my son broke something far deeper.

I had been a wife. I had been a mother. Those roles shaped my identity, anchored my purpose, and defined my world. Losing my son stripped away a part of me I did not know how to live without. I remember standing alone, the weight of sorrow crashing over me again and again. I truly believed I could not go on.

"I can't live without him," I whispered into the emptiness, my heart breaking open once more.

Those words echoed in my mind, looping endlessly, tangled with memories of his laughter, his voice, his presence. This grief was darker. It was no longer just sadness; it was suffocating. It pressed down on my spirit, pulling me into a place where even breathing felt like work. The thought of moving forward without him was unimaginable. Life no longer felt livable.

In those early days, I sank into a deep depression that consumed my thoughts and drained every ounce of energy from my body. I felt weak and helpless, like a puppet with severed strings. Memories of my son haunted me relentlessly—every cherished moment twisting into a blade that pierced my heart. I spent hours sitting alone, staring at walls, trapped in a prison of grief with no sense of time or direction.

The pain became physical. My chest tightened without warning. My breath grew shallow. Sleep abandoned me, and when it came, it brought dreams that shattered me again and again. Waking each morning felt cruel, a reminder that this nightmare was not ending, that my son was still gone.

I wrestled with guilt in ways I had never expected. I questioned every moment, every conversation, every sign I feared I should have noticed. As a mother, my instinct had always been to protect, to fix, to save. Losing my son made me feel as though I had failed at the one role that mattered most. The weight of that belief pressed heavily on my soul, whispering lies I had to confront daily. I had to remind myself, sometimes minute by minute, that love does not guarantee control, and devotion does not prevent loss.

Grief isolated me. Even when surrounded by people, I felt profoundly alone. When others asked how I was doing, words failed me. "I'm surviving" became my default response because the truth felt too fragile to share. Some days, getting out of bed felt like an act of courage. Facing another sunrise without my son felt unbearable.

And yet, even in the darkest moments, I was not completely alone.

I was blessed with a praying family who surrounded me with love, lifting me when I could not lift myself. They reminded me, gently and persistently, of the promises of faith: that God would not place more on my shoulders than I could bear. Those words became my lifeline, grounding me when I felt untethered and holding me in place when grief threatened to pull me under.

I reached for God in ways I never had before. My prayers were not polished or eloquent. Often, they were nothing more than tears, sobs, and broken whispers asking for strength. Sometimes they were angry. Sometimes they were silent. Still, I prayed. I knew I had to view my son's passing through a spiritual lens, not just through the suffocating weight of flesh and pain.

Yes, he was my son: my light, my joy, my heart. But in faith, I had to accept that God had loaned him to me. Our time together had been cut short, but the love we shared could not be severed.

My grandson, only two years old, became a living reminder of that truth. Though far too young to grasp the magnitude of his loss, he carried an innocence and resilience that astonished me. His laughter pierced the heaviness of my days, offering moments of light in the darkness that surrounded me. Through him, I saw glimpses of my son: in the sound of his giggle, in the way he played, in the love that radiated from him effortlessly.

For him, I knew I had to keep living.

I began including my grandson in my daily routines, allowing his joy to seep into the broken places of my heart. We played together, creating small adventures within the safety of our home. In those moments, grief loosened its grip just enough for me to breathe. Love had left me a precious gift: a continuation of my son's legacy.

I realized my grandson had already endured more than many adults, having lost his father at such a tender age. The thought of the road ahead for him pained me deeply, but it also ignited a fierce determination within me. I wanted to be the grandmother my son would have wanted me to be: present, nurturing, loving, and strong.

But before I could do that, I had to face my own healing.

Each day became a battle marked by both setbacks and small victories. I sought therapy, a safe space where I could confront my grief without judgment. There, I learned that healing is not linear. It ebbs and flows, just like grief itself. I learned to allow myself to feel sorrow without drowning in it. I began journaling, pouring my thoughts onto paper as a way to release the pain I carried and honor the love that remained.

Slowly, I emerged from the shadows—not healed, but breathing again.

I came to understand that my journey was far from over. My heart would always carry the scars of loss, but those scars were evidence of love: deep, powerful, and enduring. With my grandson by my side, I committed to honoring my son's memory through love, laughter, and perseverance.

Together, we were learning that even in unimaginable pain, joy could still find its way in. Grief is not a destination but a journey—one we walk step by step, hand in hand.

That verse became my beacon of hope, reminding me that even in the darkest night, light would return. I learned to cherish small moments of joy as sacred gifts, gentle reminders that love never truly leaves us. Each day, as I searched for signs of my son's presence in the world around me, I found comfort knowing that love transcends even the deepest loss.

CHAPTER 11

"Lighting the Way"

"Fear not, for I am with you; be not dismayed, for I am your God; I will strengthen you, I will help you, I will uphold you with my righteous right hand."- **Isaiah 41:10**

Time continued its relentless march forward, and as I navigated the months without my son, I grappled with the perplexing reality of grief. In those early days, each hour stretched into eternity under the weight of loss. I often felt I could not survive twenty-four hours, let alone a week. Every moment was an uphill battle, an exercise in sheer willpower. I remembered staring at the clock, counting the minutes until the day finally ended, wishing for respite from the pain that gripped my heart. Waking without my son felt like a cruel reminder that life would never again be what it once was.

Yet, as the weeks became months, I slowly began to recognize small victories along the way, moments that revealed the strength I had not realized I possessed. At first, getting out of bed felt monumental. Each day became a series of steps forward and back, moving through a landscape of emotions that shifted like quicksand beneath my feet. I wondered how I could even consider the future when the weight of the past threatened to consume me entirely. But with time, I discovered I could endure more than I had imagined. I made it through one day, then three, and eventually found I could face an entire week without collapsing under the weight of sorrow.

Those small markers, week by week, month by month, became my guideposts, quietly reminding me that healing is not a linear path but a journey of peaks and valleys. During this time, I sought refuge in prayer, whispering my fears and doubts to God in moments of solitude. I found comfort in the belief that while I felt weak and vulnerable, God was present, offering strength in ways I had not fully acknowledged. "I've got you," I felt Him say—an unspoken promise accompanying each tear shed and each laugh shared in memory of my son.

As I reflected on my own journey through grief, I realized I was not as weak as I had imagined. Each tear that fell expressed love and reinforced the bond we shared. Each memory brought fresh pain but also a flicker of warmth, pushing me forward. My faith remained the steady undercurrent through my trials, a reminder that darkness may cloud my path but light always follows. I also noticed my grandson thriving amidst our grief. He continued to find joy in simple things—a butterfly dancing through the air, the laughter of children playing, or the warmth of the sun on his face. His resilience offered a new perspective, teaching me the importance of living in the present even while carrying our losses.

Each day, as we shared memories of my son—his laughter, his love, the lessons he imparted—I discovered small sparks of joy hidden within the sorrow we carried. I learned to notice the life and love still present around us, waiting to be uncovered beneath the weight of grief. There were moments when it all felt too heavy to bear, and doubt crept in. I returned to the scripture that had comforted me so often, reminding me, *"Weeping may endure for a night, but joy cometh in the morning" -Psalm 30:5.* I became determined to seek out that joy even in the smallest gestures.

As we continued along this path of healing, I realized it was okay to have bad days—to cry, to feel lost, and to mourn. More importantly, it was vital to lean on my faith, allowing it to support me through moments of weakness. Over time, I recognized that while despair may knock at the door, it would not claim my spirit. Each small step forward reflected my strength and the enduring love that connected us all. I was determined not merely to survive but to honor my son's memory through a life filled with love, hope, and renewed purpose.

With scriptures woven throughout my journey, I found encouragement and reminders of God's promises. I began to write verses in my journal, often revisiting them during moments of solitude. *"Blessed be God, even the Father of our Lord Jesus Christ, the Father of mercies, and the God of all comfort; Who comforteth us in all our tribulation." -2 Corinthians 1:3-4*

This verse resonated deeply, reinforcing that I was not alone in my suffering.

As I embraced the journey ahead, I promised myself to keep my faith alive, seek joy in every moment, and hold firmly to the belief that God's love would guide us through even the darkest nights. I began engaging more with my community, sharing my story and listening to others who had faced similar losses. These connections fostered a sense of belonging and reminded me that grief, while isolating, could also unite us through shared humanity.

I discovered that by opening my heart to others, I could find healing not only for myself but also for those around me. Each conversation became a bond in my journey of recovery, bringing together stories of love, loss, and resilience. I learned to celebrate small victories, whether a moment of laughter with my grandson or a quiet evening reflecting on cherished memories.

CHAPTER 12

Navigating the Void

*"The Lord is near to the brokenhearted and saves the crushed in spirit." - **Psalm 34:18***

In the wake of my son's passing, each day became a challenge—a new reality where laughter felt foreign and joy seemed like a distant memory. The colors of life appeared muted, the world around me shifting into shades of gray. I often questioned how to move forward in a universe that felt irrevocably altered, as if my very existence had been torn apart.

The days blurred together in an endless cycle of grief. I would wake, staring at the ceiling, reminding myself to take it one moment at a time. The simplest tasks—a shower, a meal, getting dressed—felt monumental. I remember the first time I stepped outside since his passing. The air felt heavier, the world louder, amplifying the sorrow within me. The sun shone brightly, yet it seemed a cruel reminder of the warmth I had lost and the joy that had left my life.

Friends and family offered their condolences and support, yet an undeniable distance separated my reality from theirs. How could they fathom the emptiness inside me? Their intentions were sincere, but well-meaning phrases about time healing wounds felt hollow. How could they understand the depth of my pain without living through it? How could I convey the swirl of emotions within me—sadness, anger, confusion, and an overwhelming longing for what had been? I would simply nod at their comforting words, unsure how else to respond.

In those early weeks, I focused on caring for my grandson, still trying to make sense of losing his father. Despite his young age, he showed an intuition about grief that astounded me. One afternoon, while we sat together, his small hands fidgeting with a toy, he suddenly grew serious. "Nana, why did Daddy go to heaven?" he asked earnestly, his innocent words piercing my heart anew.

"Oh, baby," I replied, my voice trembling. "Sometimes people go to heaven to be with God, but they leave a lot of love behind. Your daddy loved you so much." I could see the wheels turning in his mind, confusion and sadness mingling in his young heart. His little brow furrowed as he processed my words. "I miss him," he said simply, and my heart broke at the honesty of his grief. In that moment, I realized that healing would not be a journey for me alone. It was one we would navigate together, hand in hand.

As the days passed, I created new routines to honor my son's memory. Each week, I made a point of visiting the cemetery with my grandson, teaching him the importance of remembering and celebrating his father's life. Together, we placed flowers on the grave and shared stories, ensuring he understood the love that transcended even the darkest circumstances. It became a sacred ritual, a way to keep his spirit alive in our hearts.

One day, as we sat in the grass beside my son's grave, my grandson pulled out a few drawings he had made. "I drew Daddy a picture," he said proudly, holding it up for me to see. The colorful crayon strokes were a tangible piece of his little heart, and I couldn't help but smile through my tears.

"That's beautiful, sweetheart. He would love it," I replied, my heart swelling with pride at the way he was honoring his father so innocently. In that moment, I realized this was not only a way for my grandson to express his love. It also reminded me of the importance of remembering and cherishing the moments we had shared.

Yet amidst the healing gestures and the rumblings of life, I often spiraled into deep sadness. It was a strange juxtaposition to witness laughter emerge from my grandson while simultaneously feeling the crushing weight of grief. The fact that my son was no longer here felt like a wound that would never heal, a gaping hole in my heart that seemed to widen with each passing day. I often felt like a ghost, drifting through conversations, unable to connect with the world around me. But I couldn't stay that way. I had to put on a brave face for my family.

I was not alone in my grief. My loved ones were grieving alongside me. My mother, too, was navigating her sorrow. I could see the toll it took on her, the light in her eyes dimmed by the weight of loss. She tried to be strong for me, yet the bond they shared was irreplaceable, and watching her struggle felt like an additional blow.

One evening, I found her sitting alone, a photo of my son clutched in her hands, tears streaming down her face. It was a heart-wrenching sight, one that made my own grief feel even heavier.

"Mother," I said softly, kneeling beside her. "It's okay to grieve. We can grieve together." I took her hand in mine, hoping to offer some comfort in our shared pain. As we sat together, enveloped in sorrow, I realized that while we each bore separate burdens, our love for my son intertwined us in a way that was both heartbreaking and healing. It was a reminder that grief, while isolating, could also forge deeper connections between those left behind.

As months slipped by, I recognized that the journey through grief was transforming me. My faith, once merely a comfort, had become a cornerstone of my existence. I began exploring scripture more intentionally, seeking verses that resonated with my struggles and offered solace. Each passage felt like a gentle embrace, guiding me through the darkness.

"The Lord is near to the brokenhearted and saves the crushed in spirit." Psalm 34:18

Those words took root in my heart, a reminder that even in my darkest moments, I was not alone. Grief was a journey that required both time and tenderness, a journey in which I would find strength I had not realized I possessed.

I began to share more openly with my friends about my struggles, letting the walls around my heart slowly come down. Those conversations, filled with vulnerability and support, became lifelines, helping me rebuild the parts of my life that had felt scattered in the aftermath of grief. I found solace in their understanding, their willingness to listen without judgment, and their shared memories of my son.

Little by little, I discovered that it was okay to laugh again, that joy could coexist with sorrow. Each day taught me new lessons about resilience and perseverance. Even in the cracks of my heart, love persisted, a reminder that life, though marked by loss, was still a gift waiting to be unwrapped each day. I learned to embrace the duality of my emotions, allowing myself to feel joy without guilt, knowing my son would want me to find happiness again.

As I moved forward, I held firmly to the belief that, although my son had left this earthly realm, he would always remain a part of me. I committed to living a life that honored his memory, one infused with love, laughter, and the understanding that every moment counts. In remembering him, I found a renewed sense of purpose, a spark to guide me through even the most difficult days ahead.

CHAPTER 13

A Legacy of Love

"For I know the plans I have for you, declares the Lord, plans for welfare and not for evil, to give you a future and a hope." - Jeremiah 29:11

As the seasons turned, I found myself navigating a new normal, one where my son's absence was a constant presence, yet the love he left behind became the guiding light on my path forward. The grief never fully dissipated. Instead, I learned to make space for it, allowing it to coexist alongside moments of joy that began to emerge in unexpected ways.

One of the most meaningful ways I chose to honor my son's legacy was by writing a book titled Breaking the Silence, dedicated to telling his story. It was a bittersweet endeavor, filled with both heartache and healing, but it was a story that needed to be told. In creating this book, I discovered a sense of purpose—a way to ensure that his dreams and aspirations would continue to shape the lives of others, even in his absence. Each word I wrote felt like a tribute, a way to keep his spirit alive.

In addition to writing, my family and I participated in the Out of the Darkness Walk each year. Organized by the

American Foundation for Suicide Prevention, the event became a powerful way to raise awareness in our community about mental health and suicide prevention. Each year, I walked alongside family members and friends, our shirts emblazoned with my son's name, uniting to spread hope and understanding. It was a visual reminder that we were not alone in our grief.

The atmosphere of the walk was both uplifting and somber. I saw the faces of others with similar stories, each person carrying their own burden of loss yet determined to bring light to the conversation surrounding mental health. As we walked together, we shared experiences, speaking candidly about our struggles and the urgent need to break the silence that often surrounds suicide. It was a cathartic experience, a chance to connect with others who understood the depths of our pain.

At the end of each walk, as we gathered to remember those we had lost, I felt a deep sense of connection with everyone there. We were a community shaped by grief, but also by hope. Hope that our efforts could lead to change, and that our loved ones would be remembered. In those moments, I felt the weight of our shared sorrow, alongside the strength that came from standing together.

My grandson became part of this tradition, his small legs carrying him beside us. He may not yet understand the meaning of the event, but watching him brought smiles from those who had known his father. "Your daddy was so brave," I would tell him, resting an arm around his shoulders, reminding him of the strength and love that would carry us forward. His innocence eased my heart, a reminder that life, even in loss, could still hold light.

Together with my mother, as we honored my son through the walk, we also expressed a clear intention to turn our grief into advocacy. Each step became a commitment to raising awareness of struggles many endure in silence. It became our mission to ensure that no one felt alone in their pain and that access to help and resources was possible, even during the hardest days. We wanted to speak for those who felt unheard and to emphasize the importance of mental health.

As the years passed, I found myself drawn to community service. In those moments of giving back, I felt a renewed sense of purpose, a way to honor my son's compassion and to create meaningful change in the lives of others. Each time I shared my son's story, I could almost hear his encouraging voice, urging me to continue. It felt as though he was guiding me, reminding me that love could be a powerful force for change.

My faith also became a steady companion through this journey. I found solace in scripture, its wisdom offering comfort and strength when I needed it most. The verses I once turned to in my darkest hours became an anchor, reminding me that even in the face of loss, light still existed.

As I reflected on the years that had passed, I recognized the depth of change within me. The grief that once threatened to overwhelm me became a force for growth, shaping me into someone more resilient, more compassionate, and more aware of the value of each moment. I learned to notice the small joys in life, the moments that often pass without recognition.

I knew the road ahead would bring challenges, but I faced the future with renewed determination. My son's legacy would live on, not only through the community work I pursued or the book I wrote in his memory, but in the way I chose to live. I committed to living with love, purpose, and a belief that even in dark times, hope remained possible. Each day became an opportunity to carry his spirit forward, to reflect the values he held dear, and to encourage others to seek help and support.

As I continued to share my journey, I discovered that my story resonated with many. People reached out to share their own experiences with loss and mental health struggles. It was a humbling reminder of our shared humanity and of how openness can create understanding and healing. I came to see that by speaking honestly about my grief, I was not only honoring my son, but also creating space for others to tell their stories.

CHAPTER 14

Embracing New Beginnings

"Cast all your anxiety on him because he cares for you."
- 1 Peter 5:7

As the months turned into years, I entered a period of quiet reflection, considering the lessons shaped by grief and healing. Each day, I woke with the weight of loss alongside a steady sense of hope. That balance became a clear measure of the life I had come to understand through experience.

The loss of my son reshaped me in ways I never expected. I often returned to memories of his laughter, the brightness in his eyes, and the care he brought into every interaction. Holding those memories became a source of steadiness, helping me move forward with intention.

I chose to embrace new beginnings and to honor my son's legacy by living with purpose and honesty. With the past firmly present, I began exploring ways to support those facing mental health challenges. I participated in community forums and joined conversations that brought attention to issues too often ignored.

My plan was to partner with local organizations and organize events centered on mental health education. The goal was to create spaces where people felt safe speaking openly, without fear or shame. What began as a plan soon became more than a mission. It became a purpose, one that allowed me to turn pain into something that could support healing in others.

The first event I helped organize was small, but its impact was clear. People showed up not only in body but with openness, sharing parts of themselves they had kept hidden for years. I remember scanning the room and recognizing that every story carried weight and every voice mattered. These gatherings reinforced a simple truth. None of us were alone in our struggles.

The community embraced these initiatives with open arms. I began receiving letters and messages from people thanking us for creating spaces of support. In those moments, I felt a sense of fulfillment I had not experienced in years. The work we were doing mattered, and in that realization, I found the courage to keep moving forward.

My mother remained a steady presence in my life. She shared in both the laughter and the tears as we adjusted to this new chapter together. On quiet evenings, we would reminisce about my son—his mischievous smile, his deep compassion, his dreams. We learned to sit with the pain without letting it consume us.

The rituals we had created, the garden we tended, the dinners we shared, and the moments of quiet reflection became lifelines. They grounded us in love even as the world around us continued to change. These small acts of remembrance connected the past to the present, providing continuity and meaning in our daily lives..

As the seasons changed, I began to see the same resilience in my grandson. No longer just a toddler, he was growing into a curious, lively boy who carried a spark that reminded me so much of his father. We continued to honor his dad's memory in our everyday lives, keeping his spirit present.

On a sunny afternoon, as we played in the park, he pointed to a passing butterfly and exclaimed, "Nana, look! The butterfly is flying to see Daddy!" The words tugged at my heart, yet I found solace in his innocent perspective—the idea that love transcends even the veil of death, that my son's spirit lived on in the stories we told and the love we shared.

These small yet profound moments reminded me that healing does not mean forgetting. It means remembering with tenderness rather than pain. It means embracing life again while carrying our loved ones in our hearts.

Reflecting on these experiences, I knew I had to continue nurturing not only my grandson's spirit but my own. I began connecting with individuals in the community who had experienced similar losses, hoping to build a circle of support where empathy could lead the way. In those shared experiences, deep bonds formed—bonds rooted in truth, vulnerability, and compassion.

As I stepped into new beginnings, I reflected on the incredible strength God had provided me through each stage of this journey. I remained committed to honoring my son's memory through advocacy, service, and love—the kind of love that endures, heals, and continues to grow.

Looking ahead, I felt a renewed sense of purpose. Life would still have its trials, and some days would remain heavy with grief. But love, resilience, and faith would guide me. The journey was far from over, but I no longer walked it in darkness. I walked with hope, light, and the enduring legacy of my son.

CHAPTER 15

Remembrance and Hope

"I can do all things through Christ who strengthens me."
- Philippians 4:13

As I stepped into a new chapter, I was enveloped in a sense of renewal that felt both liberating and invigorating. The journey through grief had transformed me. What once seemed insurmountable was now interlaced with love, remembrance, and the strength I had gathered along the way.

Each day began with a quiet promise—a vow to honor my son's memory while embracing the life still unfolding before me. I realized that healing was not a destination but a daily commitment. Some days were harder than others, yet every sunrise brought an opportunity to start again.

In the wake of my son's legacy, I felt compelled to deepen my engagement with the community. I began working more closely with local groups focused on mental health awareness and suicide prevention. Planning events, speaking to audiences, and sharing my story became acts of remembrance. In those moments, I could feel my son's presence, as if he were walking beside me, whispering, "Keep going, Mama. You're making a difference."

There were moments of hesitation, times when my voice trembled and my heart ached. Yet even through the fear and vulnerability, I felt something greater pushing me forward—a purpose rooted in love. I learned that courage often looks like showing up, even when your heart feels broken. These experiences gave my pain a new direction, turning sorrow into service.

One of the most fulfilling parts of this journey was watching my grandson grow. He was no longer a baby in diapers but a spirited, inquisitive child who asked endless questions and explored the world with wide eyes. His laughter was infectious, filling our home with a warmth I had not felt in years.

To keep his father's memory alive, we began a new tradition: "Daddy's Day." On this day, we celebrated my son's life with the things he loved most. We played baseball in the park, made his favorite foods, and shared stories that made us both laugh and cry. It was not just about remembrance—it was about creating joy in his honor.

These gatherings became a sacred ritual. Family and close friends joined us, filling our home with the comfort of shared memories. We did not shy away from grief. Instead, we made space for it, honoring its presence while also allowing room for love and laughter.

Even my mother, who once found it difficult to talk about her loss, began to open her heart again. She shared memories of my son—the way he used to dance in the kitchen and how he always brought her flowers after school. Her eyes would light up, and in those moments, I saw healing take shape.

It became clear to me that while grief never fully disappears, it can soften. It can transform into something tender and meaningful. I stopped asking why and started asking how: How could I continue to love, to serve, to honor, and to live?

The support of friends, both old and new, played a crucial role in this transformation. Their presence reminded me that I did not have to carry the weight alone. In every text, visit, or comforting word, I felt the strength of community. Sometimes healing comes in silence—in knowing someone is there, even without words.

As spring turned into summer, our vegetable garden flourished once again. We planted, watered, and watched in awe as life emerged from the soil. Each tomato, cucumber, and pepper became a symbol of persistence, a reminder that cycles continue despite our losses. Nature, in its quiet way, taught us how to begin again.

One afternoon, as we filled our baskets with fresh vegetables, my grandson turned to me and asked, "Nana, will we always come here to pick vegetables?" I smiled, brushing the hair from his forehead, and said, "Absolutely, sweetheart. This is our special place. Daddy would have loved this."

His eyes widened with wonder as he scooped dirt into his hands, laughing as it slipped through his fingers. I watched him and felt a deep sense of peace. Love had not left us; it had simply changed form.

I began to understand that embracing renewal was not about forgetting the past but about integrating it into the present with intention. It meant living in a way that reflected both the love we had lost and the love that remained. It meant finding meaning in the everyday.

Even simple routines—brushing his hair, folding the laundry, or sitting quietly with a cup of tea—felt sacred now. Every ordinary moment carried traces of gratitude. Life had slowed, allowing me to notice what I had once overlooked. Loss had given me new eyes.

Reflecting on all that had brought me to this point, I embraced the gift of each new day. The pain of losing my son would never fully disappear, but it no longer defines me. What defines me now is love, faith, resilience, and the quiet yet powerful decision to keep moving forward.

With each step, I felt more connected to my purpose. I would continue to advocate, to serve, and to cherish. My son's spirit remained a guiding light, and I would walk forward with open hands, an open heart, and the knowledge that even in sorrow, life could still bloom.

CHAPTER 16

The Shadow of March

*"The Lord is close to the brokenhearted and saves those who are crushed in spirit." - **Psalm 34:18***

As I embraced the path of renewal, I began to understand that healing does not arrive all at once. It comes in fragments— small moments of breath between waves of grief, brief pauses when life feels almost manageable again. I was learning to move forward while still carrying unimaginable loss, to exist in a world that had taken so much from me. Even as I tried to find my footing, I couldn't help but notice a shift in my mother's demeanor as the calendar edged closer to my son's birthday.

The nearer we got to March 13th, the more withdrawn she became. She spent longer stretches of time in her room, often with the door closed, leaving the house quieter than usual. At first, I told myself this was simply grief doing what grief does— resurfacing as anniversaries approach, tightening its grip without warning. After all, we were still learning to live without him. I assumed she was coping in her own way, carrying her sorrow privately, as she always had.

"I'm just a little tired, dear," she would say whenever I asked if she was okay. "Don't worry about me."

But I did worry.

I saw the sadness in her eyes, the way her smile no longer reached them as it once had. I noticed how her movements had slowed, how her laughter had softened into something fragile and fleeting. This was not just exhaustion. This was grief settling deeper, heavier, and more quietly than before.

In the weeks leading up to his birthday, she spoke of my son more often. His name surfaced unexpectedly in conversations, sometimes in the middle of ordinary moments—while folding laundry, preparing a meal, or watching television. Her voice would tremble, thick with emotion, though she always tried to brush it away.

"I'm okay, really. I just miss him so much," she would say, repeating the words as if saying them enough times might make them true.

Part of me wanted to believe her. I wanted to trust that she was managing her grief in the way that felt safest for her. But the same maternal intuition that had guided me through my own children's lives refused to be silenced. I could sense the fragility beneath the surface: the quiet unraveling of someone holding on by sheer will alone.

Grief has a rhythm of its own. It doesn't always announce itself loudly. Sometimes it simmers. Sometimes it swells slowly, building beneath the surface until it spills over in moments that feel unbearable. For my mother, March was a storm season. The memories grew louder, the absence sharper, and the weight of losing her grandson pressed heavily on her spirit.

As March 13 approached, I found myself bracing not only for my own grief but for the unpredictable waves of emotion crashing over my mother. I was still learning to navigate my own pain, and now I felt the quiet responsibility of attending to hers as well. I had hoped this year would be gentler, that we could honor his memory with a quiet moment of reflection or a small gesture of love. But the heaviness I sensed in her told me that something deeper was stirring.

Losing a loved one changes everything. It rewires the soul. It forces you to navigate a world that no longer feels familiar, one where joy and sorrow coexist in uncomfortable ways. It leaves you grasping for ways to remember while trying not to drown in the pain of remembering. Watching my mother, I was reminded that this loss was never mine alone.

She had lost a grandson—a piece of her legacy, a future she had imagined but would never witness unfold. Her grief was different from mine, but no less profound. Where I carried the unbearable pain of losing a child, she carried the quiet devastation of outliving her grandchild. It was a sorrow she rarely spoke aloud, choosing instead to shield others from its weight even as it slowly wore her down.

There were moments when I wished she would let me in more fully, when I longed for her to speak the truth of her feelings. But I also understood her silence. Strength had always been her language. Endurance had always been her response to pain. Still, I couldn't shake the feeling that something was wrong—that the silence surrounding her grief was becoming too heavy to carry alone.

I wish I had known then how fragile she truly was. I wish I had understood that sometimes strength looks like quiet withdrawal, and that silence can be as dangerous as despair spoken aloud. At the time, all I knew was that the air around us felt unsettled, like the stillness before a storm.

As we moved closer to my son's birthday, I held onto the hope that love, memory, and family would carry us through. I believed we could survive this season as we had survived so many others: together. But grief has a way of reminding us that no matter how strong we believe we are, loss continues to shape us in ways we do not always anticipate.

Little did I know that the days ahead would test us in ways I was unprepared for, dragging us once more to the edge of sorrow and resilience and leading us toward yet another loss that would forever alter the landscape of my heart.

CHAPTER **17**

Navigating the Storm

"No temptation has overtaken you that is not common to man. God is faithful, and he will not let you be tempted beyond your ability, but with the temptation he will also provide a way of escape, that you may be able to endure it." - 1 Corinthians 10:13

As the early days of March passed, a quiet tension settled over the house. The countdown to my son's birthday hung over us, heavy and unrelenting. I watched my mother withdraw further into herself, speaking less, isolating more than usual. I sensed something building, but nothing prepared me for what happened on the morning of March 13.

That morning, as I got ready for work, I noticed my niece struggling to help my mother sit up in a chair. My mother looked unwell. She was pale, distant, barely present, as if her strength was fading.

"Mother, are you okay?" I asked, trying to keep my voice steady as panic rose in my chest.

"Baby, I don't feel too good today, but I'm okay," she said softly. The tremor in her voice undercut the reassurance, revealing how fragile she truly was.

"Do you want me to take you to the hospital?" I asked. My nursing instincts were fully alert now. Something in her eyes, something I had seen too many times in others, told me this was serious.

"No, baby. Let's just get cleaned up first," she insisted. It was just like her to want to look her best, even in distress. I knew better. Her insistence felt like a delay, fear masked by dignity.

With my niece's help, we cleaned her up and helped her into her favorite blouse. I moved on autopilot, brushing her hair and buttoning her shirt, trying to hold back the dread rising in my chest. Each small action felt fragile, as if it could be the last.

When she was ready, I called 911. I gave the dispatcher every detail and asked that she be taken to the best hospital in Dallas. I was not taking any chances.

The paramedics arrived quickly. They assessed her and moved with quiet efficiency, placing her on the stretcher. I followed behind in my car, my mind racing with fear, prayer, and memory. The loss of my son was still raw, and the thought of losing my mother sent a cold panic through me.

At the hospital, we waited. The white walls of the emergency room felt colder than usual. Nurses came and went. My mother was taken away for tests and scans, and the silence around me grew louder. I was there physically, but emotionally I was reliving every moment of loss I had already survived.

Finally, the emergency room doctor walked in. His face was composed, but I could see the weight in his eyes. He had not spoken yet, but I already felt it in my chest, as if all the air had been pressed out of me.

"Your mother's condition is serious," he said. His voice was calm, but it cut through the room.

I gripped the armrest of the chair to steady myself. I was not ready. You never are. This was the beginning of another storm, one I was not sure I had the strength to endure. Still, I knew I had no choice.

CHAPTER 18

A Mother's Resolve

"God is our refuge and strength, a very present help in trouble" - **Psalm 46:1**

After my mother's diagnosis, the world around me felt unstable. Each moment brought a new surge of grief, heavy and difficult to manage. I had believed that surviving the loss of my son was the hardest thing I would ever face. Confronting the possibility of losing my mother, the woman who loved me more than anything, forced me into a state of fear and uncertainty I was not prepared for.

When we arrived at the hospital, the doctors moved quickly, ordering multiple tests and scans. Being there felt unreal. As a nurse, the environment was familiar, yet now I stood on the other side, facing the possible loss of my mother. The emergency room carried its usual sterile smell, broken by the steady beeping of machines, each sound reinforcing how serious the situation was.

After what felt like an eternity, the doctor returned with news that broke our world apart. My mother had cancer. Uterine papillary serous carcinoma, he said. It affects about twelve percent of women in the United States, but what struck me most was the reality of its late stage survival rate, often as low as zero to fifteen percent. The moment those words left his mouth, my body gave out. I collapsed to the floor, sobbing without control. It felt as though life itself had been pulled away from me.

I remember looking at my brother. His face was pale, his eyes wide with disbelief. Everything the doctor said after that faded into a wash of clinical language and grim probabilities. My mind held onto only one thought: how could I live in a world without her? She had been my constant, my strength, present through every high and every low. I had never imagined facing life without her.

As the discussion shifted to treatment options, urgency rose within me. "What can we do? Are there treatment options?" I asked, searching for any sign of hope.

"The preliminary tests suggest it may be a rare and aggressive type of cancer," the doctor explained. "We need to perform biopsies to determine the best course of treatment. Hormonal therapy could be one option, but we need more information first."

Despite the gravity of the situation, my mother remained resolute. "I'm ready," she said firmly. She was not one to shy away from challenges. Her unyielding spirit had always guided us.

"I just need to get my affairs in order," she added, her voice steady. Even in the face of uncertainty, she focused on practical matters, directing us toward what needed to be done.

My brother, always proactive, moved into action immediately, making sure my mother's wishes were honored. "We'll handle everything you need," he reassured her, his voice steady with resolve. Though he tried to stay strong for all of us, I knew he was hurting deeply as well. He never let it show. He stayed steady for her and for the rest of the family.

As we organized documents and discussed her estate, I could see that she had made peace with the diagnosis. There were no tears, no complaints, only the calm way she faced what lay ahead.

My heart ached as I watched her strength. Even then, she was still trying to support us as we moved through what felt like a long, dark passage with no clear end. It seemed she was shielding us from her own pain, wanting us to know she was ready for whatever came next.

I wanted to be strong for her, to be the anchor she needed, but worry stayed with me. I could not bear the thought of losing her as well. "Mother, you need to take care of yourself," I urged one evening as I prepared food for her.

"I'll be fine," she said, though I could sense her fatigue. "I just need to focus on getting everything in order."

As we moved forward, I began to understand that the days ahead would require patience and care from all of us. The uncertainty felt heavy, yet her readiness stirred a quiet sense of hope in me. We were a family, and we would face this together.

As the reality of her treatments became clearer, we found ourselves moving through a surge of emotions. Conversations about rehabilitation and therapy took center stage, with my mother showing reluctance toward certain options. "I don't want to be in pain," she said softly, her honesty cutting through the tension in the room.

Yet, in her refusal to pursue further treatment, my determination to fight for her and explore every possible option intensified. "Mother, let's try everything we can," I pleaded, remembering how I had once pushed her to stand up and fight through life's challenges.

She paused, weighing my words. "I'll do it for you," she replied, but the exhaustion in her eyes told another story. It was a reminder that this journey was ultimately hers to carry. After everything I had already endured, losing people without warning, my mother's diagnosis felt like a strange kind of relief. It meant there was something we could do, some action we could take to help her. I wanted to make things right, and I was not ready to lose her as well. But reality had its own limits. My mother was tired, and I could see that she was not prepared to push herself that far.

Throughout this ordeal, I remained aware that every decision needed to be guided by love and respect for her wishes. I committed to honoring her choices while making sure she knew she could rely on me, no matter how difficult the path became.

As we prepared for the unknown, I turned to my faith. I found comfort in scripture, reminding myself of God's presence in moments of uncertainty.

In the midst of it all, I relied on love, faith, and the deep connection we shared. Those anchors helped steady us as our family faced what lay ahead together.

CHAPTER 19

Trials and Triumphs

"Two are better than one, because they have a good reward for their toil. For if they fall, one will lift up his fellow." - Ecclesiastes 4:9-10

The days in the hospital blurred together, shaped by shifting emotions as we moved through the uncertainty of my mother's treatment. The steady beeping of machines and the hushed voices of nurses filled the sterile space, a constant reminder of how serious everything was. Each day carried its own weight of fatigue, worry, and quiet moments of prayer.

I often caught myself staring out the window, searching for a sense of normal life that felt increasingly distant. The sharp scent of disinfectant followed me everywhere, and I became familiar with the rhythm of the hospital: doctors making rounds, shift changes, sudden movement at the nurses' station. It felt as though time moved in two directions at once, racing forward while dragging its feet. During the quiet hours at night, I sat beside my mother's bed, listening to the steady rise and fall of her breathing. I held her hand and silently hoped her body would find the strength to carry her through another day.

As the weeks passed, I had the opportunity to review my mother's chart, and the prognosis weighed heavily on me. After discussing her diagnosis with my brother, we agreed to communicate openly about her condition, but in measured portions. I shared information gradually, enough for him to research on his own without overwhelming him with fear. I did not want to watch the hope in his eyes disappear all at once. The balance between honesty and protection became something I navigated every day. I knew he needed the truth, yet I wanted to shield him, just a little longer, from the full weight of what lay ahead. Sharing the burden in fragments felt like the only way I could cope.

"Hey," I said softly one afternoon as we sat together. "I took a look at Mother's lab results. There are a few abnormalities." I handed him the papers carefully, hoping they would help him feel included without pushing him into panic. My voice shook despite my effort to stay calm. My brother scanned the page, his brow tightening as he focused. I knew what would come next. He would take this information seriously and begin researching immediately. He had always been the fixer, the one who searched for answers and refused to give in to despair. That part of him became our anchor and our hope.

He looked at me, his brow furrowed. "What do you mean? How serious is it?" The question hung between us, heavier than I could answer in a single phrase.

"Just a little abnormal," I said, trying to downplay the severity. "It's better if you see it for yourself." I knew my brother would dive into research, looking for answers that could help him support our family. I watched as he reached for his phone, already pulling up medical articles. He didn't speak much, but I recognized his way of coping: with knowledge, with understanding, with facts he could grasp and turn into action. In his silence, I saw both his fear and his love.

I did not want to add more pain to his already heavy burden. We were both scarred from previous losses, and it felt protective to share information in fragments, letting him process the reality in his own way instead of having it thrust upon him in an emotional moment. I knew the trauma we carried—silent echoes of past grief—made this journey even more fragile. In our quiet efforts to shield each other, we found a way to move forward.

We continued navigating the uncertainty surrounding my mother's health, my brother's diligent research becoming a source of information we both relied on. Grappling with our emotions was exhausting, as we collectively bore the weight of what was unfolding while holding on to the hope that we could somehow keep her spirit alive amid the reality we faced. He would send me articles late at night, links to forums where others had walked this path, and suggestions for specialists. His efforts reminded me that we were not powerless. We were still fighting together.

My mother remained a pillar of strength, focusing on what needed to be done. "I just need to get my affairs in order," she stated resolutely, even as her struggle was evident. While it pained me to see her declining, I admired her determination to face whatever lay ahead. She began speaking more about her wishes, making sure we understood what she wanted—and what she did not. Her clarity was both heartbreaking and inspiring. It reminded us that she was still leading, still guiding us, even from her hospital bed.

One day, as we sat together in her hospital room, I received a call from my mother's best friend, who lived several hours away. "I'm coming to see her," she said without hesitation. Within hours, she and her family had driven five hours just to be by my mother's side. I was overwhelmed by the depth of that love how friendship could close distances in an instant. Her presence was a comfort we didn't even know we needed.

When they arrived, I witnessed a wave of joy envelop my mother. The hospital room, often quiet and tense, transformed into a vibrant space filled with laughter and warmth. They brought not only memories but also a new energy, reminders of better times and brighter days. For a brief moment, past and present merged, giving her something beautiful to hold onto.

"It's like no time has passed," my mother said, her eyes sparkling with a joy I hadn't seen in weeks. The moment captured the strength of their connection, a reminder of love that transcends distance and time. For that afternoon, she wasn't just a patient—she was a friend, a sister, a woman fully alive.

As they laughed and shared memories, a lightness spread through the room. While my mother had been navigating the trials of treatment, this visit provided a much-needed reprieve. I realized how vital it was for her to feel connected, to have moments that recalled life before the diagnosis. It shifted something in all of us: a quiet understanding that love could heal in ways medicine could not.

I joined them as they laughed over anecdotes from their younger days, the joy between them filling the room. My heart swelled watching the genuine happiness radiating from my mother. For a brief moment, I could set aside my worries and simply appreciate the gift of friendship and the love that persisted even in the face of adversity. Their laughter felt almost magical, a temporary antidote to sorrow.

Even in those moments, the fragility of our situation lingered. My mother's health remained a looming shadow, and occasional stillness would slip through our laughter—a shared awareness of the difficult journey ahead. We didn't speak of it, but the heaviness beneath our smiles was unmistakable.

Later that evening, I reflected on the power of family and friends to lift us even in the darkest hours. My mother's best friend reminded me of the importance of connection, of leaning on one another, and of moments that allowed us to breathe amid uncertainty. She brought more than comfort—she reminded us who my mother was beyond the diagnosis.

As the night wore on and my mother settled in for the evening, I made my way to the hospital chapel for a moment of prayer. I sought solace in God's presence, expressing gratitude for the friendships that shaped our lives and the love that had carried us through so many trials. The chapel was quiet, still. I lit a candle and whispered my prayers—not just for healing, but for peace.

With faith as my guide and surrounded by enduring love, I felt a renewed sense of hope. Challenges still lay ahead, but I knew that together, as family and friends, we could navigate the storm, embracing moments of joy alongside the shadows of grief. In those moments of connection, I realized we weren't merely enduring. We were living, loving, and finding light even in the depths of uncertainty.

CHAPTER 20

A Celebration of Love

*"How good and pleasant it is when God's people live together in unity!" - **Psalm 133:1***

As the days passed, my mother's presence in the hospital took on an unexpected lightness. Despite her condition, she found joy in small things, especially as Easter approached. There was an excitement in her voice I had not expected. "I want to look my best for Easter Sunday," she said, determination shining through. Her wish felt like a beacon of hope amid uncertainty, a reminder that even in hardship, moments of normalcy and joy could still exist. It was as if she were reaching for something familiar and comforting to hold onto.

As a nurse, I felt a twinge of nervousness. Why was she so focused on Easter? It was a day of renewal and hope, yet clouded by our circumstances. My heart raced as I watched her enthusiasm grow. Part of me knew I should stay grounded in the present, yet I also understood how important this celebration was to her spirit. Easter had always been a time for gathering, for family, for faith—a time she wanted to embrace fully despite her weakened state.

Recognizing my mother's spirit, my sister-in-law, a natural planner, came up with an idea. "Let's have Easter dinner at the hospital with mother!" she declared, her eyes sparkling with excitement. The thought of bringing a sense of celebration to the sterile hospital room filled me with hope. We quickly agreed this would be a meaningful way to honor her wishes and create a memory to sustain us through difficult days ahead. It was a chance to shift the atmosphere from illness to celebration and love.

As Easter Sunday approached, preparations began. My sister-in-law orchestrated everything: decorating the room with cheerful colors, arranging a special meal with our favorite dishes, and planning for all of us to gather together. Balloons, fresh flowers, and pastel tablecloths transformed the space. Even the hospital staff seemed touched by the warmth filling the room. Their smiles and quiet gestures reinforced that this day was different—more personal, more alive.

When Easter arrived, the hospital room was filled not just with routine sounds but with laughter and love, creating an atmosphere that felt more like home. My sister-in-law and I helped our mother get dressed. She insisted on fixing her hair, determined to look as vibrant as she felt inside. Watching her smooth her hair and adjust her clothing, I felt a surge of pride and tenderness. It was as if she were reclaiming a part of herself that illness had tried to steal.

When we sat down together, the moment felt sacred. We shared a meal filled with laughter, storytelling, and joy—a reminder that even amid hardship, we could celebrate love and family. I watched my mother smile, her eyes twinkling as she engaged with her grandkids, and for those moments, the weight of grief lifted, if only slightly. The children's innocent chatter and playful energy brought light to the room, their presence a soothing balm on weary hearts.

Looking around the room, I felt a surge of gratitude. I was thankful for my sister-in-law's thoughtful planning, which allowed my mother to feel celebrated and loved despite the challenges she faced. Being together, creating memories amid the uncertainties, felt grounding. These small acts of kindness reminded me of the strength found in family bonds, even when life felt fragile. I silently promised myself to hold onto these moments.

As Easter came and went, my mother expressed a desire to go home. "I want to be around all my friends and family," she said, her voice carrying a hint of determined excitement. Her children, grandchildren, and great-grandchildren were the light of her life, and it was clear she longed for a return to normalcy. I understood her longing deeply. It was more than a physical place she sought—it was the comfort and belonging that only home could provide. The hospital, with all its care, lacked the warmth and memories of familiar spaces.

As a family, we decided to bring her home. The day of the transition brought a mix of hope and apprehension. I was relieved she would be surrounded by family's warmth, but anxious about the challenges we would face outside the hospital. Home offered freedom, but also responsibility. We knew we would need to adjust, learn, and rely on one another more than ever. Yet there was a comforting certainty: this was where she truly wanted to be.

Once home, we arranged around-the-clock care to meet all her needs. My brother and I committed to being there for her. We would not leave her side. Even with that determination, we knew daily challenges lay ahead. We planned shifts, consulted nurses, and adapted the house to make it safe and welcoming. It was a new routine, one demanding patience, strength, and a deep well of love.

Seeing her settled in her own surroundings brought a deep sense of relief. Her favorite chair in the living room offered comfort, and the laughter of family echoed through the hallways as grandkids rushed to greet her. Familiar sounds, smells, and sights created a peacefulness no hospital could replicate. In these small details—her favorite quilt, the photos on the wall, sunlight streaming through the windows—we found healing.

Despite the uncertainty, an undeniable warmth surrounded us. We had the chance to create new memories: home-cooked meals filled with laughter, visits from family and friends that reminded her of the vibrant life she had built. Each day became a gift, an opportunity to honor the love that endured even as her body weakened. I learned to value the quiet moments as much as the joyful ones.

Navigating this new chapter of caregiving would require patience, but I was determined to honor my mother's wishes and ensure her final journey was filled with love, dignity, and the knowledge that she was deeply cherished. Her strength, even in frailty, inspired me daily. I knew the road ahead would be difficult, yet it would also hold grace, compassion, and a profound connection that nothing could break.

CHAPTER 21

Home Again

*"God is our refuge and strength, a very present help in trouble." - **Psalm 46:1***

When my mother was transported home by ambulance, a wave of relief washed over me. After weeks in the sterile confines of the hospital, returning to the comfort of home felt like a warm reprieve. As the paramedics carefully wheeled her inside, I felt a mix of trepidation and gratitude as I took in her familiar surroundings. The walls of our home, once alive with laughter and movement, now stood silent, waiting to embrace her again.

I noticed the family photos on the shelves, the scent of her lavender diffuser in the air, and the blanket she always kept on her chair—pieces of a life paused but not forgotten. Her eyes scanned the room slowly, settling on each familiar object with a glint of recognition. I could see the relief on her face, faint but unmistakable. She exhaled deeply, as if the burden of sterile lights and beeping machines had finally lifted. That moment reminded me how powerful it is to simply be in a space where love has always lived. This was more than a return to a house—it was a homecoming of spirit.

Once she was settled in her room, we made sure she had everything she needed: a glass of water, her favorite blanket, and the cherished photographs of her grandkids lining the walls. I adjusted the pillows behind her back and gently tucked the blanket around her legs. Her breathing was slow but steady, her eyes fluttering open and closed with weariness. I reached over to smooth her hair, something she used to do for me when I was a child. We placed a soft lamp by her bedside to replace the harsh lighting she had endured in the hospital. I sat beside her and read her favorite verses from the Bible to bring comfort. I knew she would find strength in God's words, so I made sure she heard them. Every detail mattered. Each one reminded her, and us, that she was surrounded by care, familiarity, and love.

"Thank you for bringing me home," she said, her voice a soft whisper filled with gratitude. Her hand reached out weakly to clasp mine, and I felt the warmth of her fingers despite their frailty. Her words were simple, yet they carried the weight of everything she had endured in recent weeks. That moment was more than a thank you. It was a surrender, a quiet acknowledgment that she was safe.

I leaned in closer and brushed a kiss against her forehead. Her eyes watered slightly, and I realized she might have feared she would not make it back. There was a quiet bravery in her voice, the kind that comes from someone who has faced pain and still chooses love. I held her hand tighter, letting her know we were there with her every step of the way. Her gratitude was not only for the physical return, but for the presence of those who loved her. She had come home not just to a place, but to her people.

"We are just glad to have you back, Mother," I replied, a smile breaking through the heaviness that had remained in the room. My voice trembled slightly, revealing the emotion I tried to keep in check. She had always been the steady center of our family, and seeing her so dependent now felt unreal. Still, I was determined to show her joy and reassure her that love had not faltered. The room was quiet, yet full of unspoken emotion. I noticed the way her face softened when I spoke, her eyes reflecting relief. I told her about the neighbors who had sent flowers and cards. I mentioned the gifts people had dropped off, each one offered with care and concern. The community that had once leaned on her was now gathering to support her. That realization made me smile, because she deserved to receive that kind of love. In that moment, I knew we would move through this transition together.

However, as the days unfolded, it became clear that my mother was no longer the vibrant caretaker we had known. She was confined to her bed, too weak to sit at the dining table or take part in the conversations that had once come easily to her. The change was unmistakable. My once strong mother, who had spent her life caring for everyone else, now required complete care herself. She could barely lift a spoon, and even speaking for more than a few minutes left her exhausted. I found myself helping with everything, feeding her, adjusting her pillows, brushing her hair. Witnessing this was painful, yet I understood it was also a meaningful chance to return the care she had once given me. Her eyes, dulled by exhaustion, still searched mine with love. When words failed her, I learned to read her expressions and anticipate her needs through quiet observation. Each act of care became a deliberate offering, a small way to ease her discomfort. Though her body had weakened, her spirit remained present, reminding me that illness does not erase identity. It changes how it is expressed.

In her weakened state, I knew it was essential to create a nurturing environment for her. When she asked for her favorite meal, I decided to make lasagna, hoping to offer comfort without the urgency that once filled our family dinners. Cooking for her felt intentional, almost reverent. I pulled out her old recipe card, the one marked with handwritten notes and smudges from years of use. As I layered the ingredients, memories surfaced of the times we cooked together, laughing over sauce stains and sneaking bites of cheese. The kitchen, once her space, now carried the quiet presence of those shared moments. I played her favorite Italian music as I cooked, hoping the sounds and smells would bring her a sense of ease. I lit a candle and arranged a small tray, wanting the moment to feel thoughtful. This was not just a meal. It was reassurance. A reminder that she was still cared for and still cherished. That lasagna carried more than flavor. It carried memory and intention.

As I worked in the kitchen, the familiar aroma drifting through the house brought a deep sense of home. I held onto the thought of sharing the meal with her. I prepared it just the way she liked, cut into small pieces and finished with a light sprinkle of fresh basil. Her favorite.

When the meal was ready, I carried the tray into her room and set it gently on the bedside table. By then, she was too weak to feed herself, so I propped her up with pillows and asked my brother to sit with her. She had requested him, wanting him close, wanting him to feed her. He took the chair beside her, and I stayed nearby, watching as he raised the fork to her mouth. Her hands trembled, too tired to assist, but her eyes brightened when she saw the dish. A brief moment of recognition crossed her face, and I felt a quiet sense of relief. She took the first bite slowly. Her eyes closed for a moment, as if taking in more than the taste alone. It held memory, care, and love in each bite.

"Mother, I made your favorite," I said softly. My voice carried warmth and quiet pride. She looked at me, her expression easing. There was a pause as she chewed and swallowed, the room holding still around us. Then she offered a faint, contented smile.

"Thank you, baby," she whispered, her voice barely above a breath. Yet in those few words, I felt everything. Her gratitude reached deep, easing the worry I had carried for so long. I touched her hand and smiled, blinking back tears.

We sat in silence, letting the comfort of presence settle in the room. Sunlight filtered through the curtains, resting softly on her frail figure. I thought of all the meals she once made for us, the ease with which she moved through the kitchen, humming under her breath. The memory felt warm and painful at once. As my brother continued feeding her, I stayed close, adjusting her pillows and offering small sips of water. I told her how proud I was of her strength. She did not respond, but the gentle squeeze of her hand told me she heard. For a brief moment, the heaviness eased. There was calm. There was peace.

However, even in those small moments of joy, I felt a deep ache within me. My mother, who had always been independent and strong, now found herself in a position that was difficult to witness. Yet she faced it with a courage that left me in awe, reminding us that she was focused on what mattered most: the love surrounding her. There was no self pity in her tone, only quiet strength. She did not complain about her limitations. Instead, she chose gratitude. I often found her gazing at photos of her grandchildren or smiling softly when she heard their laughter from another room. She would whisper kind words, tell us not to worry, and thank us repeatedly for the smallest things. Her attitude humbled me. Even when she was in pain, she tried to comfort us. Her spirit had not dimmed. It had taken on a new form, quieter but no less powerful.

During those moments, I reflected on the lessons shaped by hardship. I reminded myself that while our roles had changed, the bond we shared remained steady. It was a reminder that love can adapt and continue, even when circumstances shift. We did not need perfect days or easy conversations. We only needed each other. I began to understand that caring for her was not just a responsibility. It was a privilege. Our time together, often quiet, was filled with unspoken understanding. I learned to slow down, to listen more, and to notice what mattered. Her nods of approval, her eyes following my movements, and the way she always noticed when someone entered the room became our new language. In the stillness of those days, I found clarity. Love, I realized, does not disappear in the face of difficulty. It deepens.

While navigating this new chapter of caregiving, memories of my son stayed in the back of my mind, a quiet reminder that even in loss, love remained. I often found myself comparing the pain of then with the pain of now. Both were different, yet equally deep. The absence of my son never left me, but in caring for my mother, I began to understand grief in new ways. Watching her slowly decline brought back the ache of helplessness, the quiet mourning that comes with change. At the same time, it made room in my heart for compassion to grow stronger. I came to understand that love does not have limits. It expands, even through sorrow. My mother had once carried me through the pain of losing a child. Now, I was carrying her through her own season of loss.

I often turned to prayer, asking for strength not only for my mother but for myself as well. I would sit beside her, hold her hand, and whisper words of encouragement, reminding both of us of the quality of life we could still share. Some days, the prayers were silent, little more than thoughts held in the stillness. On other days, I read aloud from Scripture, allowing the words to fill the room with calm. I asked for patience, for grace, and for clarity when decisions became difficult. I prayed for sleep during restless nights and for steadiness in moments of fear. At times, my mother joined in, her voice faint but steady. These prayers became more than routine. They became anchors. They helped steady us when emotions rose too quickly. They reminded us that we were not facing this alone.

This verse became a quiet mantra, echoing in my mind during long nights and uncertain mornings. I recited it softly while helping her bathe, while adjusting her pillows, and when I saw her smile through discomfort. It reminded me that strength did not always look like energy or control. Sometimes, it looked like presence. It looked like showing up each day with care. That simple verse offered steadiness in moments when I felt unbalanced. It reminded me that even when I was overwhelmed, something greater was holding us together. That belief gave me the resolve to keep moving forward.

As I reflected on our situation, I became more aware of the power of connection, of being fully present for one another during times of need. Caring for my mother reflected the depth of the love we shared, a bond that guided us through uncertainty. We were no longer only mother and daughter. We became companions moving through a shared season of change. Every gesture, every gentle word, and every shared silence brought us closer. I began to see her differently, not only as a parent, but as a woman marked by resilience and grace. In time, I sensed that she saw me more clearly as well. Not only as her child, but as someone she could depend on, someone who offered comfort when she needed it most. We were both giving and receiving in unfamiliar ways. Within that balance, we found calm. We were moving through unfamiliar territory, but we did so together, guided by faith, love, and the memories we carried with us.

As time passed, my mother grew weaker. Her pain was often unbearable to witness. Some days, I had to step outside just to cry. I would call my brother and say, "I can't take this." Watching her suffer broke something in me. Yet, I knew she needed us. No matter how difficult it became, we had to be there. This was a reality no one should have to face with a loved one. At the same time, it deepened my respect for her. Even in the worst moments, my mother never complained. That quiet, enduring strength made me proud.

I knew it took a toll on my brother as well, even if he did not always show it. He stayed strong, checking on me, ensuring the family was okay. We had made a promise to our mother: we would take care of each other. And we meant it, fully, with everything we had.

CHAPTER 22

A Mother's Final Gift

"Peace I leave with you; the peace I give to you. I do not give to you as the world gives. Do not let your heart be troubled and do not be afraid." - John 14:27

As the days turned into weeks, I watched helplessly as my mother's condition steadily declined. The vibrant woman I had known and loved was fading, her once-strong spirit diminishing with each passing day. Conversations that had once flowed easily grew sparse, replaced by long stretches of silence punctuated by the labored sounds of her breathing. Each breath was a reminder of the inevitable, a countdown to a moment I dreaded.

Despite her weakness, my mother remained determined to ensure her affairs were in order. In a rare moment of clarity, she called my brother and me to her bedside, her eyes resolute and filled with a mixture of love and sorrow. I could see the strength she summoned, a final act of defiance against the illness that was taking her from us.

"I want to talk to you both about my final wishes," she said, her voice barely above a whisper. My heart sank at her words, the reality of the situation crashing over me like a tidal wave.

As a nurse, I had seen this scenario countless times, but nothing could have prepared me for the emotional weight of facing it with my own mother.

My brother, ever the pragmatist, listened intently as our mother outlined her desires—from the clothes she wanted to be buried in to the specific details of her funeral service. I, on the other hand, struggled to maintain my composure, tears threatening to spill from my eyes. I felt a profound helplessness, as if I were losing not just my mother but also a part of myself.

"I don't want you two to have to worry about any of this," she said, her gaze filled with a mixture of love and resolve. "I've made all the arrangements. I just need you to make sure my wishes are honored." Her words were a balm, soothing the raw edges of my grief, yet they also deepened the ache in my heart.

In that moment, I was struck by the sheer strength of my mother's character. Even as she faced the prospect of her own mortality, she was still thinking of us, still trying to ease our burdens and shield us from the pain of loss. Her love, unwavering and steadfast, refused to be extinguished by the ravages of illness.

My brother nodded, his voice thick with emotion. "We'll make sure everything is done exactly the way you want it, Mother," he assured her. I could see the tears glistening in his eyes, mirroring my own sorrow. We were both grappling with the reality that our mother, our rock, was preparing to leave us.

As we sat there, the weight of her words sank in. In her weakest moments, my mother remained the caretaker, determined to ensure we would be cared for even after she was gone. It was a profound gift—a final act of love that would guide us through the darkness ahead.

In the days that followed, I grappled with a whirlwind of emotions. I was overwhelmed by the gravity of the situation, yet in awe of my mother's foresight and her determination to spare us the stress of planning her final farewell. Each day felt like a gift, an opportunity to create lasting memories even as we faced the inevitable.

While my brother focused on the practical aspects of fulfilling her wishes, I was drawn to her bedside, holding her hand and whispering words of love and gratitude. I recounted stories from my childhood, hoping to elicit a smile or a flicker of recognition in her eyes. I knew the time we had left together was precious, and I was determined to make the most of every moment.

As I sat with her, I often reflected on the lessons she had taught me throughout my life: the importance of faith, the power of love, and the strength that can be found even in the darkest times. Her resilience, grace, and unwavering commitment to our family had been the foundation upon which I built my own life. I realized that her spirit would continue to guide me, even in her absence.

In the quiet moments, I held onto these lessons, finding solace in the knowledge that my mother's spirit would endure long after she was gone. She had faced her mortality with a courage that left me in awe, and I was determined to honor her legacy by living a life that reflected the values she had instilled in me. I promised myself I would carry her love forward, sharing it with others as she had shared it with me.

As the days turned into weeks and my mother's condition continued to deteriorate, I drew strength from the knowledge that she had cared for us even in her weakest moments. It was a profound gift, reflecting the depth of her love and the unwavering commitment that had defined her life. I knew that while the road ahead would be difficult, I would not walk it alone. Her love would be my guiding light.

CHAPTER 23

Saying Goodbye

*"He will wipe every tear from their eyes, and death shall be no more, neither shall there be mourning, nor crying, nor pain anymore." - **Revelation 21:4***

The final days of my mother's life were bittersweet, shaped by love and goodbye. As her health declined, we chose to remain by her side, present for the moments that remained. Each day required a balance between reflection and hope as we moved through the space between life and death. I often drifted into memory, recalling the many moments we had shared and the steady care she had always shown.

During that time, I was repeatedly aware of my mother's strength. Even as her body weakened, her spirit remained clear. She spoke often about her past, offering guidance grounded in the care she had given throughout her life. We talked about the family she built, the values she lived by, her faith in God, her care for others, and the importance of resilience. Each story brought clarity and reminded us of what she was passing on.

"Promise me you will take care of each other," she said one morning, her voice trembling but steady as she looked into my eyes. "You both need to hold onto your faith. It will guide you through every darkness." Her words stayed with me, heavy with meaning, and I felt a clear resolve to honor what she asked.

"I promise, Mother," my brother replied, a tear sliding down my cheek. I knew our time together was nearly gone, and I held onto her words as something steady. The weight of her expectations felt both reassuring and demanding, a reminder of the care that had always held us together.

The moment I feared most was approaching, yet instead of letting fear take control, I chose to focus on the care we had built as a family. I found comfort in the gatherings that continued around her, where stories were shared, laughter mixed with tears, and we supported one another. Each moment felt like an act of remembrance, a way to keep her presence with us.

On April 13, just one month after her diagnosis, the sun rose on a day marked by both light and deep sorrow. It streamed through the window as I noticed the change in my mother's breathing, now shallow and strained. In that moment, I understood the end was near, and my chest tightened under the weight of what was coming.

As we gathered at her bedside, our family stood close, offering quiet support. I held her hand and whispered words of love and gratitude. "You're going to be okay, Mom. Just hold on, please." The warmth of her skin stood in sharp contrast to the reality settling around us. The room carried a shared awareness of grief, love, and the meaning of a life fully lived.

In the hours that followed, we cried together, shared stories, and spoke our care openly. Each breath became a reminder of the path we had walked together as a family. There was deep sorrow, but there was also a calm that settled among us. My mother had guided us through many difficult seasons, and in her final moments, she brought us together once more.

As her breathing slowed and then stopped, the weight of loss settled in my chest. At the same time, memories rose with a quiet warmth. I could almost hear her laughter in the room, a reminder that her presence would remain with us. The care she gave throughout her life stayed with us, offering something steady as we faced what came next.

In the days that followed, our family remained close. We stayed connected through shared meals and time together, allowing memory to become part of our daily lives. Each gathering carried both remembrance and appreciation for my mother's life. I found comfort in the stories we told, each one reflecting the mark she left on us.

During this period, I returned often to the scripture that had supported me through the hardest moments of my journey.

"He will wipe every tear from their eyes, and death shall be no more, neither shall there be mourning, nor crying, nor pain anymore." Revelation 21:4

In the midst of our pain, I held to the belief that love continues beyond loss. I committed to carrying forward what my mother had given me, allowing her presence to guide my choices in the days ahead. With faith grounding me, I understood that this period of grief was not something I faced alone. My mother taught me that love does not end, and while the pain of losing her remained, so did my resolve to express that love through how I treated others.

As I looked ahead, I focused on honoring the lessons she passed on and living in a way that reflected them. I chose to value the moments of connection that continued to hold our family together. I came to understand that grief would take time, but it was also shaped by love, a love that would remain steady and continue to guide me.

CHAPTER 24

The Loss of My Mother

Blessed are those who mourn, for they will be comforted." - Matthew 5:4

Just as I began to regain some stability within my grief, life delivered another blow. My mother, my closest source of guidance and support, passed away nearly eleven months after the loss of my son. The timing felt relentless. It was as if loss had become a constant presence, stripping away what little balance I had managed to regain. With each passing day, a new weight settled in, and I questioned whether I would ever feel complete again or if this pain would remain part of my life.

The world around me began to feel tight and unyielding. I wondered whether I was being pushed beyond what I could manage. The scripture that once gave me comfort, "God will not place more on you than you can bear," now returned to my thoughts in a different way. I found myself caught between belief and uncertainty, asking how much more I could withstand. Grace felt distant, difficult to reconcile with the reality I was living. I searched for reassurance, for some indication that I was not moving through this experience alone.

Losing my mother felt like losing my final source of steady support. She was the person I turned to in moments of joy and in moments of pain, the one who understood me fully. Her guidance shaped how our family lived, and the reality of her absence felt unnatural and overwhelming. I had always imagined a future where she would remain present, watching her grandchildren grow and offering her guidance in quiet, familiar ways. That future no longer existed. At times, I could almost hear her laughter, a reminder of the life and warmth that once surrounded us.

When I received the news, whatever stability I had managed to build gave way. The loss arrived with force, leaving me stunned and struggling to breathe through the moment. Disbelief settled in as memories surfaced without warning, each one carrying its own weight. Grief pressed heavily on my chest, more than I believed I could endure. I wanted clarity, even briefly, something to interrupt the intensity of what I was feeling.

In the days following her death, time lost its shape. Days, hours, and moments blurred together. I moved through life on autopilot, handling arrangements with a mind dulled by shock. It felt unreal, like a nightmare I wanted to wake from but knew I could not. Life outside continued as usual while I remained stuck in a reality that felt cold and unfamiliar. I often stood by the window, watching others move through their routines, wishing I could return to something that felt normal.

Her absence made itself known everywhere. Ordinary details, a familiar scent, a favorite recipe, a photograph, triggered sudden waves of longing. I heard her laughter in my dreams, and memories of our time together surfaced without warning, carrying both comfort and pain. I missed her presence, her reassurance, her steady understanding. Grief settled in and stayed. It felt heavy, constant, and difficult to carry. I would reach for my phone to call her, then stop, faced again with the reality that she was gone. I wanted to hear her voice once more, to feel the sense of calm she always brought.

Amid the darkness, I clung to the lessons she had imparted over the years. In moments of despair, her voice surfaced within me, urging me to find strength in vulnerability and to accept pain as part of being human. Her words hovered at the edge of my thoughts, insisting that I honor the legacy of love she had left behind. Still, despite this inner guidance, I felt adrift, struggling against a tide that threatened to pull me under.

No one had prepared me for compounded grief, for the way each loss could merge with the next, creating a labyrinth both complex and disorienting. I had hoped that my experiences would foster understanding, but reality often proved harsh. The burdens I carried felt unrelenting, intensified by the question that had become a constant refrain in my mind: Why must I endure this? Why must this happen to me?

Loneliness became my constant companion as I navigated the waves of grief. Friends reached out with messages of support, yet I struggled to convey the depth of my pain. My sorrow felt too raw to share, and I often withdrew, reluctant to invite others into the chaos consuming me. On the hardest days, I felt undeserving of comfort, an unwelcome burden to those still finding joy amidst their own struggles. I wrestled with the fear of becoming a cautionary tale, a perpetual reminder of loss in the lives of others. I often cried out to the universe, searching for answers just out of reach. I longed for the words to express my feelings, to let others know how profoundly I was hurting.

Yet in quiet moments, I began to sense resilience emerging within my grief. I sought comfort in writing, translating anguish into words. I poured my emotions onto the page, shaping raw ache into clarity. I wrote letters to my mother, sharing milestones she had missed, recounting memories we had made, and reaffirming the lessons I still carried. Writing became both catharsis and homage, a way to connect with her spirit amidst the heartache. Each letter felt like a bridge to her, a means to keep her memory alive in my heart.

I also ventured into remembrance through acts that honored her legacy. I volunteered locally, encouraging young men and women to pursue their passions, something my mother had always championed. With each act of kindness, I felt a fleeting connection to her, that familiar warmth returning briefly to wrap around my heart. I began to understand that though she was no longer physically present, the values she instilled in me would continue to resonate within my being. By helping others, I was also helping myself heal, finding purpose amid my pain.

Through these acts of engagement, I discovered that love endures. Though loss weighed heavily on me, love remained unbroken, threading through my memories, reflections, and experiences. As my heart began to mend in small ways, I learned to embrace pain as evidence of the love that had filled my life. Each tear shed became a currency of remembrance, echoing the depth of my connections with my husband, my son, and now my mother. I found solace in knowing that love could transcend even the deepest sorrow, a reminder of the beauty that once was.

As I wrestle with this complex experience of compounded grief, I remind myself that healing is seldom linear. It ebbs and flows like the tide, each wave bringing both pain and solace, intermittently challenging me to confront my vulnerabilities with courage. I find myself at the intersection of grief and hope, knowing it is okay to feel the weight of loss while simultaneously searching for paths to healing. I often take a deep breath, allowing myself to take one step at a time and to feel whatever comes.

In moments of introspection, I hold onto the promise that my capacity for love will ultimately surpass the shadows of grief, guiding me through this journey. I cling to the idea that though life may never return to what it once was, I can embody the love and legacy of those who shaped my existence. With each step forward, I honor my mother's memory by integrating her teachings into my daily life. As I move ahead, I trust that it is within this balance of love and loss that I will find my way back to the light, bearing witness to the enduring bonds that continue to shape my heart. My journey is far from over, but I am learning to embrace the hope that lies ahead.

CHAPTER 25

Returning Home

And if I go and prepare a place for you, I will come again and will take you to myself, that where I am, you may be also." - **John 14:1-3**

The days following my mother's passing were a blur of somber preparations and the weight of finalizing her last wishes. Though she had thoughtfully planned every detail of her funeral, carrying out those plans was a daunting task that my brother and I undertook with both reverence and heavy hearts. Each decision felt like a step deeper into the reality of our loss, a reminder that she was truly gone.

My mother had been clear about her desires. She wanted her casket to remain open, allowing loved ones to pay their final respects. "I want to look my best," she had insisted, even as her health declined. This detail reflected her lifelong commitment to always being presentable, a trait that had defined her vibrant spirit. Her insistence brought both comfort and a pang of sadness, as if she were still trying to care for us even in her absence.

As we made the necessary arrangements, I felt both comforted and overwhelmed by the level of care she had taken. There was a bittersweet irony in the fact that even in her final moments, she was still looking out for us, sparing us the burden of difficult decisions. It reflected her love, a guiding force throughout our lives.

The day we gathered to lay her to rest, the air was thick with profound sorrow that permeated every corner of the church. Family and friends had traveled from near and far to honor the woman who had touched so many lives, their faces etched with grief that mirrored our own. The atmosphere was heavy yet also marked by a sense of unity, as if we were holding each other up in shared pain.

When I approached the open casket, my heart clenched at the sight of my mother's serene form. She looked as radiant as she had in life, her hair perfectly coiffed and her makeup applied with the same meticulous care she had always shown. It was both a comfort and a heartbreak, a final glimpse of the vibrant woman we had all loved. In that moment, memories flooded my mind, each one a reminder of her laughter, her warmth, and the countless ways she had enriched our lives.

As I stood there, my fingers tracing the delicate features of her face, the weight of my loss threatened to consume me. The realization that I would never again hear her laughter, feel her embrace, or seek her counsel was a reality I was not yet prepared to accept. Tears flowed freely, reflecting the depth of my sorrow. I felt as if I were standing on the edge of a vast chasm, peering into the darkness of a future without her.

My brother stood beside me, his eyes brimming with unshed tears. We had always been close, but in that moment, our bond felt amplified—a shared understanding of the void left in our lives. Together, we leaned on each other, drawing strength from the knowledge that we would navigate this journey of grief side by side. It was a silent promise to honor her memory together, ensuring that her spirit would continue to guide us.

When the service began, the church echoed with eulogy after eulogy, each speaker sharing a piece of the woman my mother had been. They spoke of her unwavering faith, her generous spirit, and the profound impact she had made on their lives. As I listened, I realized that her legacy extended far beyond our family. She had touched many hearts, leaving a lasting mark on all who knew her. Each story shared became part of the fabric of her life, reflecting the love she had given so freely.

As the final prayer was said and the casket closed, a wave of finality washed over me. I knew this was the last time I would see my mother's physical form, and the thought was both terrifying and liberating. She was at peace, no longer burdened by illness, and I found solace in imagining her reunited with my son, the two of them together again beyond our understanding. The thought of their reunion brought a bittersweet smile to my face, a reminder that love transcends life and death. My heart ached at the realization that I would never again return home with her by my side, her laughter and warmth filling the air as they once had. The silence felt deafening, a stark contrast to the vibrant conversations we had shared.

When we arrived at Jones Cemetery, the weight of the moment settled heavily upon us. As we gathered around her grave, my grandson reached for my hand, his small fingers intertwining with mine. In that simple gesture, I found a glimmer of comfort—a reminder that even in the depths of sorrow, life continued, and the love we shared would endure. His presence was a beacon of hope, a sign that the cycle of life moves forward, even in the face of loss.

As we laid my mother to rest, the finality of her absence settled over us like a heavy veil. The pain of losing her was a burden we would all carry, yet in the midst of grief, I found solace in the belief that she was at peace, reunited with those she had loved and lost. I closed my eyes, envisioning her smiling down on us, her spirit enveloping us in warmth and love.

In the days that followed, our family drew closer, united by shared sorrow and the desire to honor my mother's legacy. We continued to tell her stories, to cherish her memory, and to live out the values she had instilled in us. Each shared meal became a celebration of her life, each laugh a tribute to her spirit. Though the road ahead would bring challenges, I knew that with each other's support and the guiding presence of my mother's spirit, we would find the strength to navigate the journey before us. Together, we would carry her love forward, ensuring that her legacy lived on in our hearts and in the lives of those she touched.

CHAPTER 26

A New Dawn

"But they who wait for the Lord shall renew their strength; they shall mount up with wings like eagles; they shall run and not be weary; they shall walk and not faint."
- Isaiah 40:31

As the weeks turned into months, I navigated life without my mother, a journey weighed down by grief but brightened by the love she had instilled deep within me. The absence of her laughter echoed through our home, a void that felt both familiar and unbearable. Yet amid the sorrow, I began to recognize the lasting impact she had left behind, a legacy of strength, love, and unwavering faith.

My family and I honored her memory by weaving the values she cherished into our daily lives. We held gatherings, sharing meals prepared with her favorite recipes. Each bite was a tribute to the warmth she had always brought to our family table. I found comfort in cooking her beloved lasagna, the aroma filling our home as we recalled the countless celebrations she had orchestrated over the years. Each meal became a ritual, a way to keep her presence alive, reminding us of the love that had always surrounded us.

Family traditions became our lifeline, providing structure and connection amid the ebb and flow of grief. We created new rituals to commemorate her birthday, lighting candles and sharing stories that kept her presence alive in our hearts. Each occasion was filled with love and laughter, a reminder that while she was no longer physically present, her essence remained part of our lives. In those moments, I felt her guidance, encouraging us to celebrate life even in the face of loss.

As I reflected on our journey, I began to embrace the lessons learned through loss. My mother showed me that vulnerability is not a weakness; it is a bridge that connects us to one another. I found strength in sharing my struggles with trusted friends and family, allowing their support to carry me through the darkest moments. In these shared experiences, I discovered the healing power of community, a reminder that we are never truly alone in our grief.

My brother became a source of stability, and through our shared experiences, we grew closer than ever. We learned to lean on each other, navigating the complexities of grief side by side. Despite the challenges ahead, we held firmly to the belief that love could transcend even the deepest wounds. Together, we forged a path forward, honoring our mother's memory by living according to the values she had instilled in us.

These reflections resonated as I embraced the journey toward healing. They reminded me that grief takes time but can also become a pathway to renewed strength and purpose. I committed to carrying my mother's legacy forward, ensuring her spirit lived on through acts of kindness and compassion, demonstrating the love she had shared so freely with all. Each small act became a tribute, a way to honor the lessons she had imparted.

Looking to the future, I felt an undercurrent of hope stirring within me. Life would never be the same without my mother, but I was determined to honor her memory by living fully, embracing each day with gratitude, and cherishing the bonds that would guide me through the storms ahead. I envisioned a life where her teachings continued to resonate, shaping my choices and inspiring those around me.

In every breeze that rustled through the trees, in every sunset that painted the sky with hues of gold, I felt her presence. My mother was never truly gone. She lived on in the love we shared, in the memories we cherished, and in the countless lives she had touched. Her spirit was part of me, a constant reminder of the strength and resilience she had embodied.

With each passing day, I vowed to live a life that reflected her resilience, strength, and love—a life worthy of her extraordinary legacy. I would carry her memory in my heart, letting it guide me through life's challenges. In doing so, I ensured that her light continued to shine brightly, showing the way for others as it had for me. As I moved forward, I knew my mother would always be with me, a gentle whisper of love and encouragement in every step I took.

CHAPTER **27**

The Weight of Memories

"I thank my God every time I remember you."
- Philippians 1:3

As I navigate the tumultuous landscape of grief, I wrestle not only with the loss itself but with the memories that hover in every quiet moment. These memories are double-edged: refuge and torment. They anchor me to a life once full, reminding me of the love I was blessed to know, while also opening wounds I work hard to keep closed. They are both treasures and traps, fragments of time that fill my heart with warmth and comfort, yet, without warning, tear through my soul, leaving me gasping at their intensity. Each recollection carries its own shadow, haunting me with echoes of what once was and can never be again.

In the stillness of night, when the world quiets and distractions fade, the memories return with force. I can hear my husband's laughter, a sound once ordinary, now etched into my being as sacred. It plays in my mind like an old recording, so clear and vivid that it feels tangible. I see him dancing in the kitchen, apron on, a mischievous grin across his face as he stirs our favorite stew. He would twirl, dip an invisible partner, and steal kisses when he thought I wasn't watching. I would pretend not to notice, letting him think he was getting away with something. That playfulness was the rhythm of our life. Those moments, small and mundane at the time, now shimmer with significance. Each memory is like a sunbeam piercing through the clouds, briefly warming me before the chill of reality returns.

And then the grief deepens, tangled with these flashes of joy. Happiness, once so natural, now drips with ache. I remember our talks—deep, late-night conversations about dreams that never got the chance to breathe. We envisioned growing old together, taking family road trips, and arguing over what to watch on TV. All of it was simple, beautiful, and now impossible. These fragments of an unwritten future lie heavy in my chest. I mourn not just what I lost, but what we never had the chance to create. The absence of that life—the one we planned with laughter and hope cuts deeper than any wound I have ever known.

And then there is my son. His laughter was a sound that could dissolve any tension, a melody that danced through our home. I still hear it sometimes, bouncing off the walls of memory. He would drag me into the living room for endless chats. Now, that part of me is silent. Even the sight of his favorite snack or his favorite shirt in the mall sends me spiraling. These are not just objects. They are pieces of him, echoes of a vibrant spirit that now exists only in memory. I find myself reaching for what I can no longer touch, desperate to grasp the essence of who he was.

One memory I return to often is our trip to Louisiana. That vacation was more than a getaway—it was a celebration of togetherness. For weeks, we spoke of it with excitement, planning each detail. I can still see our luggage piled at the door, our son beaming with joy, unable to contain his excitement. The drive was long but beautiful: winding roads, windows down, music playing, and bursts of laughter filling the air. We sang along to old songs and argued playfully over who had the worst taste in music.

Arriving in Louisiana felt like stepping into a dream. Lush green canopies swayed gently above us. The scent of magnolias filled the air. Each day was a new adventure: tasting warm beignets dusted with sugar, exploring quirky little shops, and learning bits of history from friendly locals. We wandered hand in hand through the French Quarter, enchanted by the sound of jazz spilling into the streets, each note painting the air with joy. That city became a living memory, full of energy and light, a reflection of our family's spirit.

One golden evening stands out. The sun hung low, casting a warm glow over everything, and we found a quiet park tucked away from the bustle. My husband and son lay in the grass, pointing at clouds and turning them into animals and superheroes. Their laughter blended with the rustle of the trees, creating a harmony of love and light. I remember sitting on a nearby bench, watching them, my heart full and still. It felt as if the universe had paused just for us. I didn't know then how much I would cling to that moment, trying to preserve it, to live in it when reality became too cruel.

Now, those carefree days feel like a fading dream sweet, but edged with sorrow. They glow in my memory, but the glow is bittersweet, a reminder of what was lost. Sometimes I close my eyes and pretend I am back there, among the magnolias and music, surrounded by laughter that has not yet become a ghost. I ache to feel it all again: the sunshine, the joy, the love.

All these memories of my husband, my son, of Louisiana, of home live within me. Some are bright and vibrant; others so dark they feel bottomless. They settle over me like a cloak, sometimes comforting, sometimes suffocating. They remind me of what I had and what I now carry forward alone.

As I continue this journey through grief, I've learned that memories, even painful ones, can be a source of strength. Looking through photo albums, I don't just see pictures. I feel them. I hear the laughter. I smell the food. I sense the energy in the room. For a moment, the veil lifts. They are with me again. Love doesn't die. It transforms. It becomes the light that guides me through the darkest days.

I've made room in my life for rituals that keep them close. Lighting a candle, sharing stories aloud, making their favorite meals these small acts allow me to honor their spirits. They are my way of saying: "You are not forgotten. You are still here."

Then, just as I was grappling with the loss of my husband and son, my mother's passing struck. The weight of her absence felt like a crushing blow, compounding my grief. She had always been my anchor, the one who guided me through life's storms. Losing her felt like losing a part of myself. I remember her laughter, her wisdom, and the way she could light up a room with her presence.

The memories of our time together now feel like a bittersweet melody echoing in the chambers of my heart. I mourn not only her but the future moments we will never share—the advice she will never give, the hugs that will never happen. The grief is overwhelming, a tidal wave threatening to pull me under.

Even so, there are days when the weight of memory feels unbearable. On those days, I don't run. I let the pain come. I scream, cry, sit in silence, and wait for the storm to pass. Grief is not linear. It rises and falls like a tide, sometimes gentle, sometimes ferocious. In facing it fully, I have discovered something unexpected: fragments of resilience, a quiet strength that blooms from sorrow.

People often say that time heals. I don't fully agree. Time changes things. It dulls some edges, sharpens others. My grief hasn't disappeared. It has evolved. It no longer shatters me in every moment, but it still visits. And when it does, it brings the full color of love and loss.

Within that contradiction, I've found something beautiful. These memories—raw, joyful, and painful—are proof of a love so deep it refuses to fade. I cradle them like stones, turning them over, examining their facets. They ground me. They push me forward. They remind me of who I was when I was theirs and who I am becoming in their absence.

This chapter of my life is filled with sorrow, yes, but also with deep love. As I move forward, I carry their stories with me. I fold them into my days, into my choices, into the way I love others. In honoring them, I also rebuild myself.

Through each tear, through each shared smile remembered, I gather strength. I find peace in knowing they still walk beside me—unseen, but deeply felt. I will stumble. I will rise. And with every step, I carry them forward, wrapped in memory and held close by the power of love that endures, even after goodbye.

CHAPTER 28

Emotional Distress and Seeking Help

*"Carry each other's burdens, and in this way you will fulfill the law of Christ." - **Galatians 6:2***

In the wake of losing my mother, I found myself submerged in a sea of emotional distress. Waves of grief crashed over me with alarming frequency, each one revealing deeper currents I had not previously fathomed. I often felt like I was treading water in a vast ocean, struggling to stay afloat while the waves pulsed relentlessly around me. Navigating this reality was a challenge I had never anticipated, and every day felt like a battle against an unrelenting tide.

The emotional fallout from these losses was complex and multifaceted, manifesting in ways I struggled to comprehend. Some days, I felt overwhelmingly sad, held fast by the shadows of despair that surrounded me. Other days, sudden bursts of anger surged through my veins like a fever. I did not know whom to direct that anger at God, the universe, or myself for not preventing these losses but I felt its intensity consume me, raging against the inconceivable weight of it all.

In my quieter moments, I experienced a profound sense of loneliness that settled like thick fog, obscuring the light of hope. Friends would check in, asking how I was doing, and while I knew they meant well, each inquiry felt heavy, burdening me with the pressure to perform normalcy. I would force a smile, saying "I'm okay," but inside, I was a chaos of pain. I found it difficult to articulate the complexity of my emotions, the entanglement of sorrow layered atop the grief already festering in my heart.

The weight of silence can be suffocating. In the early days of grieving, I wore my sorrow like armor, heavy and stifling, yet invisible to the outside world. I believed that enduring the pain alone was proof of my love for her. But grief, when left unspoken, grows denser. It seeps into mundane moments: a half-made cup of tea abandoned on the counter, the way I would catch myself dialing her number before remembering. The isolation was more than loneliness. It became a distortion of reality. Without an external anchor, my grief turned into a hall of mirrors, reflecting only anguish and guilt.

One of the most confusing aspects of this emotional turmoil was the uninvited guilt that often accompanied my grief. I would lie awake at night, tormented by thoughts of inadequacy, wondering if I was honoring my loved ones properly and whether I was allowed to grieve deeply while also searching for joy in life. There were moments when I would laugh, and almost instantly, a wave of guilt would crash over me, making me feel as if I were betraying their memory.

Each decision became fraught with uncertainty. Should I resume the activities I once enjoyed? Was it disrespectful to allow myself fleeting moments of happiness while the weight of grief still lingered? I felt like an intruder in my own life, hesitating at the threshold of joy, uncertain if I would ever truly belong in the world again. The pressure to "move on" and find closure felt like an impossible expectation, and I often recoiled from it, wishing instead to dwell in the memories of those I had lost.

Seeking ways to navigate this emotional distress, I turned to cooking and baking. Preparing meals and experimenting in the kitchen offered temporary relief, a distraction from the chaos in my mind. I poured my heart into every dish, allowing the scents of herbs and spices to envelop me, if only for a moment. Yet even as I found solace in cooking, those moments were often tinged with sadness. The kitchen had always been a sacred space shared with my mother, filled with her laughter and sage advice that seemed to linger in the air. Every dish I prepared was a bittersweet reminder of her presence. I could almost hear her guiding me through the steps, teaching me the secret ingredients to add, as we had done countless times before.

In those moments, I felt a duality of emotions comfort intertwined with deep longing. Creating her favorite recipes brought me a sense of closeness, allowing me to relive memories of the two of us chopping vegetables or preparing holiday feasts. Yet the same act also dredged up feelings of loss, the stark reality that those days were gone forever. Cooking with my mother had been a union of love, and each meal I prepared became a delicate homage to our bond, layered with both memory and grief.

I found solace in the profound realities that arose from our shared experiences—the recognition that grief is a universal language transcending individual circumstances. With each story shared, I witnessed the resilience of the human spirit, the raw strength that emerges when we confront pain together. These moments reinforced my understanding that healing can emerge from the connections forged in the darkest places.

Amid the emotional chaos, I also sought refuge in nature. Long walks became my respite, a way to engage with the world beyond my mind. As I strolled through parks or wandered trails, I found peace in the rhythm of my footsteps. The gentle rustle of leaves underfoot reminded me that life continues in its own way. I would often pause, inhaling the fresh air, allowing myself to be fully present, listening to the world around me. Nature offered a calming presence, a refuge amid the emotional tempest, reminding me that life ebbs and flows.

It was in these moments of introspection that I realized emotional distress is not simply a downward spiral. It is a complex mix shaped by love, memory, and resilience. As I navigated the waves of sorrow, I began to notice strands of hope woven through my grief. While the pain remained real, so too did the love that endured beyond loss, serving as a guiding light through my darkest hours.

Through it all, I learned to be patient with myself. Each tear shed is not a sign of weakness but a reflection of the love I carry for those I have lost. I embraced the idea that grief is not something to overcome but a journey to navigate one that evolves in phases, sometimes requiring retreat inward, while at other times prompting me to reach outward and seek connection.

As the waves of grief continued to crash over me, I realized that navigating this journey alone was not sustainable. Vulnerability carries its own strength, and seeking help is an act of courage, not weakness. The emotional landscape shifted beneath my feet, and the burden I carried felt lighter when shared. I hesitated, wary of imagined judgment and unsure of the steps I needed to take to find my way forward.

Eventually, I realized I could no longer struggle in silence. Encouraged by the whispers of friends and the advice of support group members I had met along the way, I took the step of seeking professional help. I began attending therapy— a decision that initially filled me with both trepidation and hope. The prospect of exploring my pain felt daunting, but perhaps it was exactly what I needed: a compassionate listener who could guide me through the chaos and help me uncover the hidden corners of my grief.

The first session stirred a mixture of emotions. I entered the therapist's office feeling both apprehensive and relieved. I sat in a comfortable chair that smelled faintly of lavender. She greeted me with kindness, her gentle demeanor inviting me to share. As we began to talk, I found myself hesitant, struggling to find words to express the weight of my heart. What would I even say? How could I begin to untangle the complexity of my experiences and emotions?

But as the session unfolded, something shifted within me. I began to speak, lifting the veil of silence that had suffocated my voice for so long. I shared the stories of my loved ones and how their absence felt like an open wound. I described the weight of grief and the emotional turbulence within me. With every word, I felt pieces of that weight lift, as though I was finally exhaling after holding my breath for what felt like an eternity.

Therapy became a sanctuary where I could unpack the layers of grief without fear of judgment. I soon discovered that grief, in all its complexity, is a journey uniquely tailored to each individual, often filled with unexpected twists and turns. My therapist helped me recognize that my experiences of pain, sorrow, and even fleeting moments of joy were all valid parts of a larger whole shaped by love and loss.

We explored coping mechanisms to support my healing journey, from mindfulness and meditation to journaling and creative expression. I learned the value of grounding myself in the present moment, using techniques to quell the waves of anxiety that frequently threatened to pull me under. At times, the emotions surged—anger, sadness, despair but having tools to navigate these waves became invaluable.

In discussing my past, I began to confront not only the losses but also the isolation that had long plagued me. I realized that, for much of my life, I had buried my emotions beneath layers of resilience, often dismissing my own needs to support others. This revelation marked a turning point. It allowed me to see that asking for help was not an act of weakness but a courageous acknowledgment of my humanity. Grief does not have to be a solitary journey.

During our sessions, I also began to recognize the importance of community. I sought out local support groups where individuals facing similar losses gathered to share their stories. These meetings became a sanctuary, offering understanding and connection among those who truly comprehended the weight of grief. Listening to others articulate their experiences helped me feel less alone. The shared tears and laughter fostered a profound camaraderie, and I quickly realized that our collective pain created a bond that words could not capture.

The act of seeking help is not merely about alleviating pain; it is about reclaiming your life. Therapy provides a structured environment where you can confront your grief and articulate feelings that often feel too heavy to bear alone. It offers a safe space to explore the complexities of loss, helping you understand that grief is not a linear process but a winding path with highs and lows.

During this period of emotional exploration, I also sought out support groups where others shared their stories of loss and heartache. Relating to others in a circle of understanding felt like a balm to my soul. In those spaces, I discovered that grief is not a burden to carry in isolation. Listening to others reminded me that I was not alone in my suffering. We shared our stories, embraced vulnerability, and offered comfort to one another as we navigated this difficult path.

Support groups taught me that healing is a communal act. At my first meeting, a widow shared how she had screamed into pillows until her throat burned. Another man described planting a tree for his son, whispering apologies to its roots. Their raw honesty dismantled my shame. I realized I was not failing at grief; I was human. Psychology shows that communal mourning rituals lower cortisol levels and foster resilience.

One group session stands out in my memory an evening filled with warmth and camaraderie. We formed a circle, each person recounting their stories with varying tones of honesty: some spoke with laughter amidst tears, others barely managed a whisper. As I listened, I felt a sense of solidarity, a collective understanding that filled the room. When it was my turn, my heart pounded, but I began sharing snippets of my journey, making sure to include the love I still held for my husband, son, and mother.

With each story shared, I noticed the faces around me nodding in understanding. Empathetic smiles and encouraging remarks created a space where I felt heard and validated. Hearing others' experiences made me acutely aware that love persists beyond physical presence, flowing through shared stories and memories. Realizing that connection can thrive even amidst loss added a new dimension to my healing process.

In these healing spaces, laughter sometimes surfaced through the weight of sorrow, easing the pressure of grief. At times, shared anecdotes led to quiet laughter, shifting the pain into something more manageable and allowing joy to exist alongside sorrow. We celebrated the lives of our loved ones by recalling their quirks and moments that mattered most to us.

As I continued seeking help, I came to understand that healing from grief does not mean forgetting those I loved. It means allowing their legacy to remain part of my life. With guidance from my therapist and encouragement from the support group, I began forming intentional ways to remember them, ways that honored the love I shared with my family while still making room for my own growth.

Through therapy and the support of this community, I started to rebuild my sense of self. I was no longer defined only by loss. I made space for joy, hope, and recovery. I learned to hold grief and laughter at the same time, shaping a form of resilience grounded in love, memory, and strength.

As I take each step forward, I understand that seeking help is a courageous act and a way to connect with others who carry grief alongside me. It has broken the isolation I once felt and opened space for healing, compassion, and understanding. The road ahead remains uncertain, but I find steadiness in knowing I am no longer moving through it alone.

This chapter is still unfolding, with lessons emerging over time. I remain committed to listening to myself and honoring the legacy of those I loved most. Each day, I take deliberate steps toward healing, supported by the love that continues to surround me and remind me that hope can exist even within grief.

As I reflect on my life, I see emotional distress as an inherent part of the human experience. It shapes awareness and builds insight that can be shared with others facing similar struggles. While challenges remain, I move forward with the understanding that hardship can lead to healing and growth. Grief has reshaped me. It has shown me that vulnerability is strength and that love, even when marked by loss, can form a steady base for resilience.

As I take each step forward with intention and grace, I trust that grief, in all its complexity, will continue to guide me through this journey. With every scar, I carry the lasting imprint of those I loved, a steady reminder of their presence as I move through life, holding both the pain of loss and the enduring beauty of love.

CHAPTER 29

Embracing the Journey

*"For his anger lasts only a moment, but his favor lasts a lifetime; weeping may stay for the night, but rejoicing comes in the morning." - **Psalm 30:5***

The journey through grief feels like a constant movement between hope and despair, a rhythm that leaves me both uplifted and exposed. When moments of resilience appeared, brief and fragile, they were often followed by sudden setbacks that pulled me back into sorrow. I wanted a direct path toward healing, a clear road to acceptance and peace. But grief does not move in straight lines. It shifts and changes, offering its lessons in ways that are rarely predictable.

After months of therapy and support group meetings, moments of clarity began to surface. On some days, memories of my loved ones brought warmth instead of pain. I caught myself smiling at small reminders of them, songs, scents, shared jokes. Each memory carried love and nostalgia without overwhelming sorrow. In those moments, I felt myself returning, slowly and deliberately, piece by piece.

On brighter days, I walked through the park, breathing in the crisp air and watching spring flowers push through the soil.

Each bloom felt like a quiet promise. Life continues, even when you feel trapped in darkness. Journaling helped as well. I recorded the highs and lows, letting my emotions spill onto the page without judgment.

But grief does not release you easily. Just when I thought I was making progress, an unexpected trigger would surface. A familiar melody. The scent of my mother's perfume. An empty chair at dinner. Any one of them could send me spiraling. The pain surged like a wave, stealing my breath and pulling me back under. Shame followed quickly. I felt embarrassed for not being "over it," as if grief came with a deadline.

The loneliness in those moments felt suffocating. Silence magnified my thoughts until they spiraled inward. Shouldn't I be stronger by now? Will I ever feel whole again? What if I am stuck here forever? One night, I sat alone holding a family photograph. It felt vivid and final. We were laughing in that image, living without awareness of how brief it all was. The tears came then, sharp and unrestrained.

But in that raw anguish, I remembered what my therapist had said. Grief is not a problem to solve. It is an experience to carry. Slowly, I learned to stop resisting it. The setbacks were not failures. They were proof of love that no longer had a place to go.

I began building small rituals to steady myself. On difficult mornings, I brewed my mother's favorite tea. When panic tightened in my chest, I walked without a destination, relying on movement alone. I volunteered at a community garden, pressing my hands into the soil and remembering how my husband loved growing tomatoes. These acts were not replacements. They were connections between then and now.

The setbacks still come. A holiday, a scent, a turn of phrase can arrive without warning. But now, I meet them differently. I let the tears fall. I light a candle. I say their names quietly. And when the wave passes, as it always does, I stand up again.

Because grief is not the opposite of healing. It is part of it. This journey has taught me that loss creates empty spaces within us, but those spaces also allow resilience to take shape. Though my husband, son, and mother are gone, the love we shared remains. It shows up in the way I tell their stories, in the meals I still prepare, and in the quiet kindness I offer strangers because they would have done the same.

As I move between heartache and healing, I reflect on the difficult path grief has carved through my life. Each stage has revealed the strength of the human spirit, shaped by sorrow and moments of joy. The experiences that weighed heavily on my heart also revealed the depth of love and memory, reminding me that healing is not an endpoint. It is a process marked by both clarity and pain.

Grief is not linear. It moves in unpredictable ways, carrying sudden emotions and hard earned lessons. Progress often walks alongside pain, yet even despair carries insight and reminders of the love that still lives within me. I have learned that while loss shapes us, it is our ongoing connection to those we have lost that strengthens us and helps us move forward.

The absence of my husband, son, and mother weighs heavily on my soul, yet I have learned to understand my grief through a spiritual lens. They were never truly mine. God entrusted them to me for a time, and I find comfort in believing they fulfilled their purpose in this life. Their time here, though brief, was sacred, and I have come to accept that God called them home, despite the pain I still carry. This belief has become a steady source of comfort, reminding me that love endures and that their presence continues to guide me as I move forward.

To anyone navigating grief, I want you to know that your feelings are valid. When the weight becomes overwhelming, remember that seeking help is not weakness. It is courage. Whether through therapy, support groups, or honest conversations with people you trust, sharing your burden can ease the strain and reveal paths toward healing that grief often hides. You do not have to walk this road alone. Connection can offer relief, strength, and space to breathe again.

Healing unfolds in unexpected ways, through laughter alongside tears, through warmth drawn from memory and the ache of longing. Allow space for both emotions to exist together, understanding they do not cancel each other out. Grief is complex and uneven. Let it reflect the depth of love that has shaped your life. Love does not end with physical absence. It continues through memory and through the strength you slowly build.

Setbacks along this journey may feel overwhelming, yet they also hold the possibility for growth and change. Even in moments of vulnerability, you are reshaped by experience, not defined by it. Each scar carries meaning, echoing the love you hold and the resilience you continue to develop. Give yourself permission to feel every part of grief, knowing you are not alone in this process.

As time passes, I encourage you to honor the memories of your loved ones in ways that feel meaningful to you. Create your own rituals of remembrance, whether through journaling, cooking their favorite meals, or finding solace in nature. Carry their presence with you as you continue living your life. Allow their love to guide you in moments of darkness and offer direction as you move toward healing.

In quieter moments, when the world feels heavy and shadows press in, remember that it is okay to pause and breathe. Allow yourself stillness. In these moments, you can reconnect with the love that remains. Let memories surface, not as a source of pain, but as reminders of the joy they brought into your life. Each recollection holds meaning, reflecting a bond that continues beyond time and distance.

As I navigate this winding road, I have learned to celebrate the small victories—the moments when laughter breaks through the clouds of sorrow, when a familiar song brings a smile instead of tears. These instances remind me that joy and grief can coexist and that it is possible to honor my loved ones while still embracing life. I have come to understand that bouncing back from setbacks is not about erasing the pain but integrating it into the story of my life.

With each passing day, I strive to cultivate resilience and find strength in vulnerability. I remind myself that healing is not a race. It unfolds gradually, requiring patience and self-compassion. I have learned to be gentle with my heart, allowing space for grief in all its forms. Whether I am joyful or sorrowful, both are valid experiences that shape my journey.

As I stand on this evolving path, I embrace the duality of my existence. I am both a survivor and a bearer of love, capable of feeling joy and sorrow, worthy of embracing the full spectrum of my emotions. Each setback tests my strength, yet I emerge with renewed purpose, carrying the knowledge that love transcends loss.

In the months ahead, I will continue to honor the delicate balance between grief and hope. I will cherish the memories that nourish my heart while welcoming the growth that emerges from my experiences. As I bounce back from each setback, I will find comfort in the belief that resilience is an integral part of my existence, a reflection of the love that remains within my soul, guiding me toward healing along the journey ahead.

To anyone in the depths of grief, know that you are not alone. Embrace the journey with all its ups and downs, and trust that healing is possible. Allow yourself to feel, to grieve, and to love fiercely. In doing so, you will discover the strength within you, the power to rise again, and the beauty of living, even in the face of loss.

If you're walking this road too, I won't tell you it gets easier. It doesn't—but it becomes different. The weight remains, yet you learn how to carry it. You will find your own ways to bend without breaking, perhaps through music, nature, or helping others who ache as you do.

Most of all, remember: Grief is not a detour from life. It is proof that you loved deeply. And that love does not disappear.

It transforms. It becomes the hand that pulls you forward, even when the path is dark.

So, breathe. Feel what you need to feel. And when you're ready, take the next step—not away from the pain, but through it. You are still here. That matters.

EPILOGUE

As I stand at the crossroads of remembrance and renewal, I am acutely aware of the patterns running through my life—the vivid moments of joy interspersed with the shadows of grief. Losing my husband, my son, and my mother was among the hardest experiences I have ever faced, yet it has also been a profound teacher, guiding me through the complexities of love and loss.

In the wake of her passing, I have learned to carry her spirit within me, reflecting on the values she instilled: love, compassion, and resilience. Each day reminds me to cherish the connections we hold dear, to celebrate the lives we have lost, and to honor their memories by living fully and authentically. I have come to understand that grief is not only an ending but also a beginning—a catalyst for growth and transformation.

Through our family gatherings, I find solace in sharing stories that evoke both laughter and tears, keeping my mother's legacy alive in every shared meal and joyful moment. Her strength continues to inspire me, and I remain committed to fostering the bonds of love that unite us. These gatherings have become sacred spaces where we reflect on her life, ensuring her spirit remains a vibrant part of our family story.

Life moves forward, filled with both challenges and triumphs. Each day brings its own gifts, a reminder that hope can flourish even from the depths of sorrow. I carry her with me, knowing that while we may be separated by physical distance, the love we shared connects us forever. This love fuels my determination to embrace life fully, to seek joy in small moments, and to extend kindness to others, just as she would have done.

As I look to the future, I do so with an open heart, ready to embrace every moment, knowing that love, once given, remains a lasting force in our lives. I am committed to living in a way that honors her memory, allowing her spirit to guide me as I navigate the journey ahead. In this way, I find comfort in believing she will always be a part of me, encouraging me to live boldly and love deeply.

NOTE TO READERS

Dear Readers,

As you take this journey with me through the pages of my story, I invite you to walk beside me as I navigate the intricate tapestry of love, loss, and resilience. This book is more than a recounting of events. It is a heartfelt exploration of the experiences that have shaped my understanding of grief, family, and the enduring bonds we share.

In sharing the story of my husband, my son, and my mother, I hope to illuminate the complexities of moving through life while carrying unimaginable heartache. These profound losses have tested my spirit, yet they have also revealed the strength that can emerge from vulnerability and from the unwavering support of family and friends.

I write this not only to honor their memories but also to offer comfort to those who may be walking a similar path. Even in the darkest moments, I found glimmers of hope that reminded me that love allows us to endure, heal, and eventually celebrate the lives of those we cherish.

I am deeply grateful to my family and friends who have stood by me, lifted me up, and reminded me of the importance of connection during the most challenging times. Your love has been a guiding light. I truly hope that readers of this book find not only empathy but also inspiration in the shared human experience of loss, healing, and embracing life's precious moments.

Thank you for allowing me to share my story with you. May it remind you that you are never alone in your struggles, and may it encourage you to cherish the love that continues even beyond loss.

With love and gratitude,

Tonya Jones

ACKNOWLEDGMENT

In Loving Memory of Jibriel

Your gentle spirit and unwavering love were the foundation upon which our lives were built. Though our time together was cut short, the memories we shared will forever be etched in my heart. Your kindness, your laughter, and your steadfast commitment to our family continue to inspire me each day. Until we meet again, may you rest in eternal peace. I love you forever.

With love, your wife.

In Loving Memory of Deterrious "DJ"

My son, my shining light, your infectious joy and boundless curiosity brought such vibrance to our lives. Though your time with us was far too brief, the love we shared will echo through the generations. Your spirit lives on, guiding us with its gentle warmth and reminding us to cherish every moment. You are forever in our hearts. Mama loves you, my son.

With love, your mother

In Loving Memory of Mother

The matriarch of our family, your unwavering strength and steadfast love were the cornerstones that kept us grounded, even in the darkest of times. Your wisdom, your laughter, and your steadfast faith inspired us all. Though your physical presence is now gone, your essence continues to shine through in the lives you touched and the legacy you have left behind. We will forever be grateful for the gift of your life. I will always love you to the moon and back.

With love, your daughter

ABOUT THE AUTHOR

Tonya Jones was born and raised in Sterlington, Louisiana, and currently resides in Cedar Hill, Texas. She served as a Hospital Corpsman in the United States Navy and has over 15 years of experience as a nurse, specializing in various areas of healthcare. Her career in nursing was fueled by an unwavering desire to help others, a passion that has defined much of her life. However, it is her role as a mother that has had the most profound impact on her journey. The tragic loss of her son, DJ, transformed her in ways she never could have anticipated.

As a medical professional, she spent years saving lives, yet she was unable to save the one that mattered most: her own child. The weight of that loss, coupled with the guilt and pain, became an unimaginable burden, one that she hopes no other parent will ever have to endure.

Through this book, Tonya seeks to honor DJ's memory and bring awareness to the silent struggles of mental health. She hopes that by sharing her story, others will feel encouraged to speak up, seek help, and understand that mental health challenges should never be faced alone. Her journey of grief and healing has deepened her passion for suicide prevention and mental health advocacy, leading her to support other families navigating the complexities of loss and healing.

Tonya continues to channel her pain into purpose, advocating for mental health awareness and encouraging open conversations about the realities of grief. She carries DJ's light with her in everything she does, ensuring that his love, his story, and his legacy live on. She lives with her family, cherishing every moment, and using her voice to bring hope and healing to others who need it most.

www.ingramcontent.com/pod-product-compliance
Lightning Source LLC
Chambersburg PA
CBHW051202120626
46547CB00012B/1165